MEN
MAGNIFYING
MANHOOD

GIVING HOPE
&
EMPOWERMENT

VOLUME 2

MEN MAGNIFYING MANHOOD

GIVING HOPE
&
EMPOWERMENT

VOLUME 2

CALVIN ELLISON, PHD

Copyright © 2019 by Calvin Ellison, PhD

Ordering Information
Quantity sales. Special discounts are available on quantity purchases by corporations, associations, and others. Orders by trade bookstores and wholesalers. Please contact Dr. Ellison at dr.calellison@gmail.com

Editor
Lita P. Ward, The Editorial Midwife
LPW Editing & Consulting Services, LLC
Editorial Midwife Publishing
www.litapward.com

Publisher
Published in the United States of America by
Ellisons Consulting Services LLC

ISBN: 978-0-578-56482-1

ENDORSEMENTS

August 8, 2019

To Whom It May Concern,

Just like his previous work Men Magnifying Womanhood, Volume 1, Men Magnifying Manhood, Volume 2 delivers in all the same ways. With a diverse collection of men writers, this book provides stories of struggle, strength, perseverance, and triumph for any man in any situation. This book arrives at a crucial time for society as it helps redefine masculinity in a modern age.

Sincerely,

Honorable Senator Dr. Donzella James, District 35
121-D State Capitol Atlanta, Georgia 30334
District: (404) 625-8855
State: (404) 463-1379
E-mail: Donzella.james@senate.ga.gov

COMMITTEES:
Interstate Cooperation, Chairman Special Judiciary, Vice-Chairman Economic Development and Tourism Education and Youth

"Dr. Ellison is inspiring, challenging, and educating men to know God's expectation of men in their homes, community, and at work. Read this book, and join the movement of Men Magnifying Manhood!"

Timothy Brown, National Vice President of Strategy
Black Data Processing Associates

Dr. Calvin Ellison's genius framework of real stories written by real men to encourage other men and help them find silver lining among dark clouds of life!

Uzma Khan

Dr. Ellison has been instrumental in the health community with uplifting and encouraging men to share their experiences. Such as the title, men giving hope and empowerment is highlighted to share common themes and an outlook on life. Oftentimes, men may not be as vocal with expressing challenges and how to overcome obstacles. This book is enlightening with demonstrating the journey from each story on how to achieve success in life.

Phenomenally,

Angela Perry, CEO
CODE W LLC

I find that this book is very valuable and much needed, for all men of all races and ages in this present time. So many men suffer from identity crisis as in who they are and what does it mean to be a man. This book like Dr. Ellison's previous books is a valuable tool and resource for helping men understand their role in today's ever changing environment. I highly recommend this book written by this anointed man of God.

Orlando Nelson, INFO LLC

Dr. Calvin Ellison is such a resource to the community. He provides knowledge and wisdom in the most critical areas of a man's life. I'm very happy to work closely with him as we both serve in the leadership of the Atlanta Black Chambers. He is definitely one of the foremost thought leaders in the realm of physical, mental, and spiritual health. This book is a gift to all of us. We've been so challenged in this process as males who need to realize our full potential.

It's time to Magnify Manhood!

Melvin M. Coleman, MBA
Executive Director

Atlanta Black Chambers
384 Northyards Blvd N.W.   Office 877-964-6222 ext. 101
Bldg. 100   Cell 678-548-5242
Atlanta, GA 30313   www.atlantablackchambers.org

Men Magnifying Manhood should be a part of anyone's library. When GOD said let us make man, Dr. Calvin Ellison heeded the call. Man is more than just flesh and blood. The complete man is mind, body and spirit. Dr. Ellison, an anointed man of GOD, and his contributing writers have contributed spiritual insight in the areas of what it takes to magnify the manhood of men. Attributes such as maturity, responsibility, discipline, and commitment are just a few of the areas which he shares insight. This read should inspire the Prodigal sons in the community to return home and assume their rightful place as leaders in the home and the community. Remember, Knowledge is the new Currency. A must read!

Calvin Maddox
VP Business Development
Atlanta Black Chambers

Dr. Calvin Ellison now gives an inspirational look at the philosophy of Men Magnifying Men. Man is both material and spiritual and this book is a marvelous combination of the two. This book will lead men to self-respect while helping one to distinguish between self-respect and self-conceit.

George G. Hill
Centers for Disease Control and Prevention (CDC)

The book, Men Magnifying Manhood by Dr. Ellison is timely and much needed material by every man who desires to maximize his destiny.

Dr. Festus Adeyeye
General Overseer
Abundant Life Christian Center Worldwide

CONTENTS

FOREWORD

Men Magnifying Manhood, Volume 2 is a book dedicated to the betterment of men. Because no one is perfect, there is room for all of us to improve in one area or another of manhood. However, we need mentoring, guidance and tools to help us. This book gives you some of all three.

Whether you are trying to know what a man should be, what a man should look like or how a man should carry himself, you have in your hand an ideal resource. Regardless of where you are in your quest to maximize your manhood, embrace hope and be encouraged that you are not alone.

None of us have arrived, but you have in your hand the stories of men who have given you this book as a point of reference and a lifestyle guide so that you will be empowered, so that you can own your truths and be the best version of yourself.

Chad Anderson
Executive Director
African American Male Wellness Initiative
Aawalk.org

In today's ever changing society, men find it an overwhelming task to identity, find purpose or position in the home and the larger community. God designed boys to learn from their fathers on how to be a man, a brother and a friend. Manhood is synonymous to RESPONSIBLE, DEPENDABLE and COURAGEOUS. In the absence of fathers in our community, it is essential, critical that men find guidance and direction in the areas of day to day life, survival and responsible living. It has been easier to just step away from the task (the responsibility) at hand. Dr. Calvin Ellison's book is a dependable and secure source of advice, guidance and perspective. A complete read for today's man from men who have shared their lives with the intent of giving hope, guidance and empowerment. It reveals and chronicles the lives of men from various backgrounds, experiences and professions. These men share their beginnings, strengths, struggles, insights, and solutions. It's written by men and for men, whether married or single, to help every male be a better man, father, professional, leader and community contributor to human progression. These testimonies serve as a reminder of what goodness, determination and faithfulness creates in the life of men who will embrace these attributes.

Michael Gamble
Senior Radio Manager
CLI Media, Inc.
(404) 465-3388 (ATL-office)
(478) 239-4540 (New Media-office)
(404) 720-0967 (direct)
www.newmediadirectatl.com

INTRODUCTION

Every living thing was designed to have a conception, evolutionary process and maturation. As humans God created us to be His representatives, for the purpose of His pleasure and have stewardship over what is visibly seen (Psalms 8:6). As males, God's intention for us is to emerge from the womb, be nurtured, molded and led into manhood; with all its roles and responsibilities for the maturation for males.

But wait a minute; there is a problem! Many homes have no father in them. Countless males have no men to mentor them. Hurting, uncared for and confused boys roam our streets and fill our jails, longing to be guided in to true manhood. The desire is in them to be real men because God put it there. A male's greatest fulfillment comes from being the man God created him to be.

This book is the result of a group of men who said, "Enough is enough! We will come together. We will work together. We will deal with why many males never experience the Promised Land of meaningfulness, maturation and manhood. We will shine the light of our collective experiences, education and evolutions to make the journey of life brighter for every male we possibly can."

Hence, you have in your hands: "Men Magnifying Manhood, Volume 2."

~ Calvin Ellison, PhD

GOD MAGNIFYING MANHOOD

Genesis 1:26

Job 7:17

Psalm 8:4-6

Biography of Calvin Ellison, PhD

Calvin Ellison, PhD is an Apostle, Author, Naturopathic Doctor, Certified Nutritional Consultant, Radio Host, Global Wellness Trailblazer and Marriage and Men's Advisor. He is the Founder of several Networks: the Kingdom Advancers Network of Churches and Businesses, Heirs Together Marriage Enrichment Network, the Vibrant Living Group, and the Men's Empowerment Network. He has also served on the Farmville, NC Economic Development Council, the North Carolina Institute of Medicine Committees, the North Carolina Mental Health Task Force and the Community Outreach Network Board of Eastern North Carolina.

While pastoring for 20 years, he is a constant presenter at Community Colleges, Universities and Businesses on various topics from Health and Wellness, Community Engagement, and Personal and Professional Growth. He has worked with such groups as the NC Office of Minority Health and Health Disparities (as its State-Wide Coordinator of two Health Programs), the Town of Farmville, NC as a Health Consultant, the National Kidney Foundation, the Health Start Foundation, North Carolina Department of Health and Human Services Women's Health Branch, Health Departments, Community-Based Organizations and Local Churches.

Dr. Calvin Ellison is the author of five books and co-author of five national publications. Together he and his wife have ministered in ten different countries. They have been married for 36 years and have three children and seven grandchildren.

Personal Profile

Key Words

Beyond, Create, Innovative, Wow, Imagine

Favorite Quote

"Making things happen to create new realities."

Values

Equitable Relationships, Networking, Empowering Others, Changing the Status Quo, Visionary Thinking

Marketable Skills

Public Speaking, Organizing, Leading, Networking, Continued Learning

Contact Information

Email: dr.calvinellison@gmail.com

Website: www.doctorcalvinellison.com

LinkedIn.com: Dr. Calvin Ellison

Facebook: Facebook.com/calvin.ellison.39

RESPONSIBILITIES OF MEN

Calvin Ellison, PhD

Since the first time I read the above quote, it continues to intrigue me. I believe every man was created to be responsible. The Bible shows us that. Adam was put in the garden with responsibilities. *And the Lord God took the man, and put him in the Garden of Eden to dress it and to keep it.* (Genesis 2:15)

Adam was not put there to sit around, eat grapes, and let the wind blow through his hair while he just gazed at the clouds all day. He wasn't even put there to be on his knees under a tree somewhere praying all day. Ouch! I know that probably touched a Christian who has had the wrong concept of what God wants out of us.

After being created in God's image and blessed with the words: *be fruitful, multiply, replenish, subdue and have dominion*, he was given responsibilities. God's Words were not intended to just make us spiritual (in some people's cases spooky); they are to empower us to be responsible. God is responsible. Jesus was responsible for our redemption. The Holy Spirit has His roles of responsibilities in our lives. The angels have their responsibility. Everything God created has some measure of responsibility. Birds, flowers, trees, bees, the sun, the moon and stars, the clouds and rain – everything has responsibilities.

Whatever you receive from God has responsibilities attached. Your life, health, relationships, skills, talents, and abilities all were given with responsibilities attached. Irresponsible men are costing society far more than any sickness or disease, accident or war could ever cost. As a matter of fact, irresponsible men are often the causative factor of the above problem. A major learning in life is learning what to be responsible for and how to carry out that responsibility.

Adam was told what to be responsible for – the Garden. Then, I believe that when God would visit him in the Garden (Genesis 3:8), He would give him instructions on how to be responsible for what was placed under his care. Listen to me brothers; don't get married until you have been instructed on marriage and how to take care of a woman. The lack of what I have just said has led to more family and societal problems than we have time to discuss in this chapter. Possessions and pleasures without an understanding of responsibilities have often led to disasters. Adam was given instructions on how to take care of the garden and his wife. Never accept responsibilities without getting the instructions on how to be responsible.

If there is any class we need a refresher on regularly, it is the class of being "Responsible with Responsibilities." The first to attend the class should always be us – men. Always! A man can never truly love himself, his wife and family and what is in his world until he has been instructed on how to be responsible. Let's not talk about "love" until we have talked about responsibilities. Don't get it twisted. You will love to the degree that you understand how to be responsible. Many of marriages have ended in divorce, not for a lack of love, but for ignorance or neglect of responsibilities. Who then hurts? Everybody; the man, the woman and children, society, and the whole world.

If the measure of a man is his ability to accept (and fulfill) responsibility, then we need to know what being responsible means and increase in being responsible. Webster's dictionary defines responsibility as being dependable, keeping promises and honoring our commitments. It is accepting the consequences for what we say and do. It also means developing our potential. People who are responsible don't make excuses for their actions or blame others when things go wrong.

You aren't expected to be responsible until you have accepted the responsibility, made the promise or given your commitment. Once you do, you are responsible. You should not catch an attitude when someone puts you in check about your actions. To do so will dimish your influence and weaken your impact. Be responsible for your gardens. Keep your promises and follow-through on your commitments. By all means, don't let someone have to keep reminding you on what you committed to. Do your do! Be on top of your game. Do what you are responsible for and do it well. The late Dr. Martin Luther King, Jr. said if you are going to be a street sweeper, be the best. The foundation to great people is an understanding of what it means to be responsible.

We are the ones pushing ourselves forward or holding ourselves back. The power to succeed or fail is ours. This is one of the reasons I like David in the Bible. He was a responsible young man before he became King of Israel. He was responsible taking care of his father's sheep while no one was watching him. A responsible person will do what they have to do whether others are watching or not. He was responsible to lead, protect, and make sure they were fed. Because he was faithful with his resposibility to care for the sheep, God was going to give him the opportunity to lead his people.

Before David would have opportunity to lead a nation, he had to deal with a problem that had been blocking the nation's progression. The problem was called Goliath. The giant stood in the way of the nation's progression, requesting the nation to send him a man to fight against him. Even Goliath was looking for a man from the Israelites to take the responsibility to fight for the nation. No one volunteered. Not even two or three of them together volunteered to be responsible for the nation. These men were like many men today. They were content looking cool without being responsible. They had titles without turf. They wanted publicity and noterioty without performance. They didn't have the experience of fighting a lion and a bear to be proved faithful over a responsibility given to them. But David did.

It is wise to be proven responsible over small things before going after larger opportunities. Don't seek to be popular, but those who seek popularity over prudence often end in disaster. When David saw Goliath, he saw an opportunity to display his resposible habits. People who have been responsible seek greater opportunities to be more responsible. Irresponsible people just look and talk about problems while responsible people do something about problems. The foundation of David's promotion as king was his willingness to accept responsibility for the well-being and progression of the nation. Men look for opportunities to be responsible while boys look for opportunities of pleasure and prestige.

Now let's look at some areas that we as men are responsible for. Keep in mind that if you are responsible for something you will have to respond or account to who gave or permitted you to have the responsibility. Knowing who have to account or answer to someone should help keep your attitude and actions in check. But here is a causative factor to the failure of many men. The attitude that I am my own man, I don't have to answer to anyone. Wrong! Tell that to your boss or landlord. Tell that to someone you borrowed money from or someone who lent you their vehicle. Number one, we are responsible to our Maker. You didn't get on earth by yourself. The Sovereign God assigned you to be here. You are here on purpose with an assignment to do something, solve a problem or problems and help earth be a better place. You didn't fall from the sky as an alien or evolve from a monkey. Ask your parents. They will tell you that you didn't come through the womb of a monkey. As a matter of fact, you could not have gotten here without them. A few months ago, I read an article about a "nut" who was suing his parents for giving birth to him without his permission. How stupid! On top of that, he was going to sue his parents of whom both of them are attorneys. I don't know where he bumped his head, but wherever he did, he left some of his brains there.

You cannot fulfill your manhood without being responsible to God Who created you. A ball player cannot max his or her skills out on the field or court without being responsible to the coach and the team. Neither can you maximize your manhood without consulting with your Creator. Since when does a product know how to be all that it can be without the knowledge of who created it?

The first responsibility of every man is to be responsible to God Who made us. We are to be responsible to the Presence of God. This means we should seek to abide in His presence on a daily basis by seeking after Him through His Word, meditating on and protecting what He has said. In simplier terms, communicate and consult with Him daily. Seek His wisdom and guidance about your purpose and life matters. He wants to be your consultant, coach, mentor and leader daily. He wants to help us in everything. The best athletes engage in ongoing coaching. Successful business people talk regularly with consultants and people who make a difference in life seek the mentorship of those who have been impactful.

Adam was placed in the Garden of Eden. It was Eden where God met with him. Eden in shorter terms means the place of the manifested presence of God. So Adam was to abide in the presence of God. As men, we cannot be all we were created to be without the presence of God. We need God like the earth needs rain. We need God like fish need water to live, grow and develop in. Plants were designed to grow in the ground and you and I were made to grow from the rich, soul of the reality of God.

A second responsibility of man is a garden. A garden is something we are responsible for. Adam was responsible for the Garden of Eden. In other words, there were works that God assigned him to. God gave him work before he gave him a wife. No man has any business marrying a woman without having work, a job, a business or an assignment he is working on and developing first. Typically we don't start out owning a business, so we then are given a job opportunity to get started in developing ourselves. Every man needs work. How you handle a job given to you will reveal how you would handle your own business. Do you show up on time? Do you do a thorough job at work? Do you have an accountable attitude? Do you seek to please your boss? Are your breaks longer than they should be?

Every man must find his work. Your work or garden of responsibility is deposited in your purpose. Purpose speaks to why you are on earth. Keys to your purpose are understanding about your passions, desires, and what problems you seek to solve for humanity. I was not purposed to discover what is in the seas. I have no intererst in deep sea diving. I don't even like being on a boat unless it is about the size of a cruise ship. I love the beauty of tall buildings, but have no desire to be educated on how to design one. I definitely don't have a desire to climb up the side of one to clean windows. Not the kid! But I am passionate about human development and progression. I love educating people on how to have a healthy body and a successful marriage. I am turned on aobut building teams. What turns you on? What drives you? What do you keep thinking about even though you aren't doing it right now? Answering these kinds of questions will cause you to find your purpose, your calling, your passions or your garden.

The third responsibility that I believe man has is to love his wife. Of course, you have to be marrried to love a wife. A girlfriend is not a wife. Shacking up with partner is not a wife. A woman on the side is not a wife. If you are married, you have the responsibility to love your wife above and beyond everyone else on the planet. This includes your mother, sister(s), friends or whoever. When you said "I do" you made a major commitment to God, your wife, your family and her family and even the world at large about what kind of man you would now be.

You honor God by how you deal with the institution of marriage that He created. You please God by how positively you treat the woman He allowed you to have as a wife. You affect and influence the family that you gave her, to your leadership and care by the way you love her. Lastly, you get to model the love of Christ toward the church by the way you treat your wife. Ephesians 5:25-32, says, *"Husbands, love your wives, even as Christ also loved the church, and gave himself for it; That he might sanctify and cleanse it with the washing of water by the word, That he might present it to himself a glorious church, not having spot, or wrinkle, or any such thing; but that it should be holy and without blemish. So ought men to love their wives as their own bodies. He that loveth his wife loveth himself. For no man ever yet hated his own flesh; but nourisheth and cherisheth it, even as the Lord the church: For we are members of his body, of his flesh, and of his bones. For this cause shall a man leave his father and mother, and shall be joined unto his wife, and they two shall be one flesh. This is a great mystery: but I speak concerning Christ and the church."*

So how can we love our wives? Let me talk about some ways:

➢ Love her by gaining knowledge about the institution of marriage (and of course continuing to gain more knowledge). At the time of this book, I have been married to my "girlfriend," my wife for almost 37 years. It seems like it was just yesterday that we got married. As I look back over the years, I believe I could have been a better husband, especially in the earlier years had I had more information about the institution of marriage before we said "I do." We often think about the bride and the wedding and have little information about marriage itself. Think about this; it is the wedding that is the gateway to the bride men desire to have. But further, we walk with the bride into a non-physical place where both of us will spend our spiritual, emotional, and mental lives – the marriage. It has its own set of standards and operating instructions just like any other institution.

➢ Love her through knowledge. The Apostle Peter was given a great piece of advice for husbands in 1 Peter 3:7. The first part of that verse instructs husbands to live with wives according to knowledge. He is telling us to get knowledge about them. Talk to her parents about who she is. Get all the information you can from them. Listen to her brothers and sisters if she has any. Talk to her extensively about her likes, dislikes, passions and pursuits. The more you know, the better you can serve and lead her. Don't forget to observe her closely. You will learn a lot through simple observation.

> Love her like the model man loves his wife. Who is the model man? Jesus is and He has a wife called the Church. The above passage in Ephesians Chapter 5 reveals this. Well, how does Jesus love his bride? First, He has knowledge of her. He loved us when we didn't have the desire or capacity to love Him back. He loves us so gracefully and mercifully with our imperfections while helping us become better people. He loved us enough to give His life for us, knowing we can't pay Him back or ever come close to loving Him the way He loves us. I hope you catch my flow. There are so many other expressions of the way He loves His people that I don't have time to discuss. Just keep praying that He opens your understanding more about how He loves His bride. He will do it.

The final responsibility of man I want to discuss in this chapter is continual personal development. Life is all about evolving. We are conceived and begin to grow in the first environment, the womb. After we have maxed out in the womb environment, we are birthed and then placed in a crib environment. There we continue to grow and develop and eventually are taken out of that environment and given more space to continually grow and become.

Notice that in either of the above environments, you weren't there long. You don't hear of a baby being in the womb for two years. It is not normal for a young child to be in a crib for three years. The only time you see such a thing is on a comedy show. Why? Because all things being equal, growth is expected at certain intervals. We expect the child's weight to change, height to change, countenance to change and vocabulary to change. We don't want our children talking "dada and mama" at sixteen years of age. They shouldn't be carrying a milk bottle to school in a bag at 12 years of age. Growth requires change. Maturity demands development. Continual development is a must for men expecting to be more influential and impactful. Keep on reading and studying. Keep on following mentors. Keep on subjecting yourself to challenging opportunities. Live with the concept of being comfortable with the uncomfortable. A greater version of you will slowly emerge.

~Dedication~

Maurice Shackelford

Calvin Deon Ellison, Jr.

Kenneth Battle, Jr.

Titus Fozard

Justin Knight

Jacob Best

Deangelo Jamal Ellison Gray

Shawn Taylor

Antonio "Popcorn" Ellison

Terry Pugh

Tyrone Duckett

Eric W. Smith

Keon Reid

Jason McFarlane

Emmanuel Thomas

Kevin Sheppard

Johnell Gibbs

Mal Williams. Jr.

Willie Dixon

Melvin Coleman

Biography of Chad Anderson

 **Chad Anderson** is the Executive Director of The National African American Male Wellness Initiative also known as AAWALK. Before that, he was and is the Director of Team Elite Six Multi Media Firm. He is also a part of various annual campaigns with initiatives such as Barbershop Talk to address mental health, Cooking with Dads, a 5k walk/run, and children's pavilion.

The **AAWALK initiative** is dedicated to changing the health disparities among African American men by providing free annual health screenings, access to community resources, and education on living a healthy lifestyle. In 2018, he and his team hosted over 50,000 attendees and screened thousands of black men.

Barbershop Talk Initiative...Real Men...Real Conversations. The goal of this project, which is a mental wellness initiative, is to bring together barbers and wellness professionals to help facilitate conversations for black men in our community. It is also designed to break the stigma attached to addressing mental health issues and stressors for black men. This project provides a safe space for men to be venerable and talk through life challenges, at the same time walk away with real life solutions that empower their lifestyle.

Cooking with Dad is an initiative that brings fathers and children together to learn about healthy eating habits. The team creates partnerships with local African American chefs to provide hands-on demonstrations and education on making proper food choices and relevant cooking via trainings, awards, and accomplishments. This project provides children with a good point of reference, with their fathers making healthy meals.

Chad's lifestyle consists of having as many great experiences as possible. His areas of focus are spirituality, family, and career/business. The lifestyle includes fashion & style, culinary, travel business & economics, health and wellness. His mission is to provide the same experience, knowledge and access to those seeking; to empower their own life and the style in which they live it.

Personal Profile

Key Words

Empower - Educate - Serve - Lifestyle

Favorite Quote

"I've never met a strong person with an easy past." ~Atticus

Values

Spiritual Relationships - Family - Career – Community

Marketable Skills

Sales, Partnership Development, media production, Project management - Content Development for Black Culture

Contact Information

Websites: www.teamelitesix.com, www.aawalk.org, canderson@aawalk.org, chad@teamelitesix.com
IG: tes_yourself
Telephone: 614-648-9720

The Life & Times of a Black, Single Father Executive

Chad Anderson

I was a middle child who grew up in a single parent household. As a middle child, and only male in the family, I considered myself a loner; I wasn't young enough to be babied and spoiled, but I also wasn't old enough to be relied on and roll with the big kids. Oddly enough, this experience also forced me to emerge as a leader in peer circles. Not having a father in the home made it challenging to know what a man (a real man), father and husband should look like. Throughout my life, many mistakes were made because I lacked information and a point of reference that reinforced good decision making. Still, I carried myself as though I knew it all to mask the ignorance that lied inside.

As a 7-year-old, I was molested by an older cousin which led to isolation, introversion and difficulty freely expressing emotions. This happened again when I was 12 years old at the hands of a 25-year-old babysitter. I believe these experiences have impacted my experiences and relationships with women. As a young adult, sex was used as a coping mechanism for depression, anxiety and insecurity. After some self-reflection, I learned that I have used sex

17

as a way to feel value and validation. I created a false value of myself by the number of women I was intimate with. This led to toxic relationships and children with women who do not share my same values.

Because I was homeschooled, I had more flexibility than most. When I was done with school work, I was allowed to spend time at my Grandfather's pawnshop where I met hundreds of people and developed the ability to understand different personality traits and body language. It involved a lot of negotiating through sales, buying and trade deals made in this environment. This exposed me to what it was like to be a business owner and this is where I developed my entrepreneurial spirit. This put me in a space to where I could start my first business. My sophomore year of high school, I started a cell phone and pagers store. During that time activations could happen by phone so none of the agents knew my real age. When I turned 18, the industry began to be consumed by larger cellular corporations and I found myself too small to compete. I knew I needed to transition into something else, so I explored and met my friend and who I consider a mentor, Will Walters. I learned a lot from him. At 19 years old, Will brought me in on a project where I assisted increase brand awareness for African American organizations through grassroots marketing. Soon those efforts turned into a boutique urban marketing team developing co-branding opportunities for main stream brands to engage with African American audiences.

My efforts as a team leader on those projects led to becoming circulation and distributor for C-Magazine/Columbus based lifestyle magazine. Mr. Walters launched Monarch Magazine, a national lifestyle publication and I was able to enhance my marketing and sales experience through participating within event experiences. This was the start of my passion for marketing and promoting lifestyle driven experiences. It taught me how to segment target audiences out, how to create proposals, leverage and develop partnerships, raise funding and most importantly, how to navigate complex processes. I eventually moved to Washington, D.C. where there is a large African American population which led to me being immersed in black culture at its finest. I was exposed to what I did not see in Ohio, including exposure to thriving African American corporations and nonprofit organizations.

This experience helped me build business acumen, learn how to manage relationships and fundraise. It also put me in a space to identify what I'm good at and passionate about. I knew I wanted to work in a space that allowed me to positively impact lifestyles in the black community. Years later, I started my own marketing company called TES Media. We are focused on creating digital, print and event content for black culture. This eventually led me my current role as Executive Director of the African American Wellness Initiative in 2016. The goal of the National African American Male Wellness Initiative is to raise awareness for preventable health diseases that kill African American men. We are focused on spreading the message that living a healthy lifestyle is about taking a holistic approach to maintaining good health and good health is maintained through healthy habits.

When I came on board with the initiative, we had approximately six cities and in three years, we expanded our market to 16 cities. Now we have been able to not only have a footprint in these markets, but also forge alliances with major corporations. One major highlight of my career is spearheading the creation of the official AAWalk show in collaboration with DSW and New Balance. I helped to negotiate this historical deal because I was able to structure it to where they have created a customized shoe without an athlete attached to it. DSW has also now come on board as a shoe distributor and they have 500 stores in the United States alone. Our shoe isn't just a shoe. It will grow into something so much more. It's been great to be a part of something that is changing the narrative about black men and showing that young black boys capable of doing and being able to change and the community that raised me. Years before this moment, I identified health and wellness as an area of passion. Now, I am spearheading a movement that will have a large impact on the urban community.

I really didn't even acknowledge it or even bring it up in my life until I was an adult because my cousin, who was a male, made it more difficult to deal with. As a black man, I have learned that we really don't like to talk about childhood trauma. Another challenge happened when I was 12-13 years old when a babysitter began to sexually abuse me the day my mother and step dad went on their honeymoon. But once again, as black men we don't talk about these things because they are still taboo in our culture. I think these experiences played a role in shaping my life as it relates to being a parent. From there came my second challenge, being a single father of five. I have four biological children and adopted one, my friend's son.

Being that my sexual experience was prematurely started, I really did not take responsibility for how I handled women. As an adult I have realized these things. I then began to make sure quality time was spent with my children and having custody of them began; in my own way, to break that cycle of those things that happened to our black children all too often.

I think my other challenge has been having a felony on my record. Although I learned how to make significant amount of money, I never really educated myself on how taxes work. I have learned the lack of information led me to not filing taxes properly which also led to being convicted. Anytime you owe over $1,000,000 in taxes to IRS, you get a felony from that! At a young age, I was unknowingly conditioned to make financial decisions based off emotions, not based off of logic.

At any time, I could allow these challenges and choices to define me. Instead these experiences shaped me to be the man I am today. I have allowed the things that I'm dealing with now to mold me in to a better version of myself. I have also been able create a better point of reference for my children to live by. Mistakes are your best teacher.

The meaning of manhood starts from self-love. This means parents have an important responsibility to instill this quality in their children. This also helps prevent us as black men looking for validation, through how many women you slept with, how much money you have, what type of clothes you wear or car you drive. I believe that those are signs of insecurity. Manhood means being a father who can not only provide the basic level of needs such as a roof over your children's head, food, clothing and education, but also talking with them to see how they feel about the things in life. And find interest in what they're learning. For me, the silver lining in life is everything! Meaning that you're paying attention to the subtle things in order to have a big impact. I say that because I've learned from being a father in raising children you get better results when you make your child feel like they are making their decision for themselves even if it's at the adolescent age. It is important to have good communication with your children. A father must be able to humble yourself and get down to their level so you can understand them and they can understand you. I believe that's what a real man does because it's easy to just tell a child you do this because I said so. But it's different to ask a child why did you do that or why do you think that that was right or wrong. Being able to have engagement and build trust with your children are extremely important in ensuring they are prepared for life.

Manhood is being able to take spiritual counsel and discipline from the elders in your community. So often we feel like no one can judge us except God. However if we have spiritual wellness in our life, we're open to take advice and counsel and be humble enough to serve our community for the betterment of being an example.

I believe manhood is one that can follow and still be a leader as it relates to career, fatherhood, and community. As an executive or boss, it is easy to direct an employee to do this or that. But when you allow a person to contribute their own input, you are allowing them to take ownership of your project. Now, you're starting to expand who you are as a man because your priorities and your desires are not just for personal gain, but at this point, there is gratification for success of the team's effort. You're willing to get your gratification, your roses at the end and allow your team to shine. The moral is putting other's interests before yours; making sure your team/family is taking care of. To me, that is manhood.

The best advice I could give to men and our young black kings is always be the smallest person in the room. Make sure you're the one who knows the least, because it's the only way we can really grow; being around people who have more information and think bigger. Don't get me wrong! It feels good to be the smartest person in the room because it seems to others that you know everything. But you only find yourself knowing more than the person next person. But if you force yourself to go be the little guy in the room, you can learn and step up your game to another level.

Often I am asked, "Why do you do what you do?" To answer that question, I like using this analogy: I feel like my service is like filling the ocean with a teaspoon. The work that I do is important, but it's also a big job. Oftentimes, one may believe that I am not making an impact because the job is so great. But one teaspoon at a time, I will get the job done. I know that every ounce of energy I put into what I do is affecting somebody else, whether I know them or not. For example, the free screenings we offer, the digital content created, the print and event information have allowed men to know their health numbers, see a doctor annually and get active in the community. Every year we have men go from our screening area directly to a hospital because they found out they were sick. I'm proud to say I have helped save manhood every single day. And for that I am blessed.

~Dedication~

Jordan Courtright

Robert White

Kim Anderson

Rick Hameed

Will Walters

Kevin Parish

Tim Johnson

John Gregory

Andre Hill

Perry Gregory

Joe Black

Biography of Jaishawn Betts

Jaishawn Betts is a 14-year-old young man, born to a teen mother in Omaha, NE on Jan 14, 2006. Jaishawn truly desires to have a relationship with God. He enjoys making people feel good about themselves, reading and editing videos for people's entertainment. Jaishawn Betts is a member of Love and Faith Church in Snellville, GA and an up and coming ninth grader. His desires and goals are to one day join the Marines, move to New York, be an ordained minister and have a happy family. He strives to be the positive example for his three brothers and a sister. Jaishawn is the epiphany of a successful young African American male in America.

Personal Profile

Key Words
Precise, Accuracy

Favorite Quote
Everything you go through has a reason behind it.

Values
Family, Good Work Ethics, Treating People Well

Marketable Skills
Communicating, Writing, Repairing Electronic Items

MY TESTIMONY AND MY STORY

Jaishawn Betts

My name is Jaishawn Betts, the youngest new member of the Men Magnifying Manhood Movement, and this is my story. Born Jan 14, 2006, I do not remember much until I was six years old. At that early age, I struggled with anger problems. Whenever someone would try to be my friend, I would tell them to shut up or leave me alone. I believe the only reason I had anger problems is because I was being bullied at the time. I was scared and assumed others were going to bully me, so I bullied them first. Later, I evolved from anger to sadness, otherwise known as depression. I would go home from school crying. Every day I would run in my room, take a shower, clean my room, and go to sleep in my bed. My mom suspected something was going on at school and it was. I was being bullied by everyone I had given a chance to be my friend. During this time, my only friends were my mom, my teacher and my brothers.

One day, my brother Jordan and I went outside to play. While we were playing, we ran into my bully. We tried to avoid him, but

27

he caught up with us. His older cousin was with him and he was stronger than us. I was seven years and my brother was only five. My bully was around nine and his cousin was about thirteen years old at the time. The bully kept talking badly about my mother trying to get me to talk about his mother. I resisted until they started to bother my brother. Out of anger, I called both of them some curse words. Shocked, they looked at me and punched me in the face. I started to cry and my brother Jordan became angry too and tried to beat them up. I told him let's just leave and go home, but my brother insisted on beating them up. He ran up to one of them, punched one of them from the back and ran home. At the time my auntie was living with us, so when we went arrived home, we told our mom and auntie that we were punched by two bullies. My mom and auntie insisted that we go to their mothers and tell them what had happened. My mom confronted the mothers of them and the kids got in trouble. After that, we went home, ate dinner and went to bed. However, as usual, I cried myself to sleep.

Years later, the same things were happening at school. I continued to be bullied and not make any friends. Now it was because my mother couldn't afford to buy me Jordan's and name brand clothes. We had to wear what we had, and kids made fun of me because of that. Once middle school started, I became very depressed. I tried to commit suicide by taking multiple pills. The pills weren't mine, butt my mother's Benadryl pills. Shortly thereafter, I found out that my mother was also struggling with depression which made me more depressed. I didn't know how to help my mom, because I was going through the same thing I was and I didn't know what to do for myself. So, I went to school and yelled out to my teacher, "I'm going to hang myself!"

All of the teachers surrounded me, showing so much love and concerned. That me even sadder that the teachers didn't want me to harm myself. My mom didn't want me to kill myself and I was the only one who wanted to die. I thought that if I died, it would be more peaceful and everyone would be happy without me. I still tried to go through with it. I went to my room and cut myself. But, I got scared that my mother would be really hurt if I killed myself. So, I stopped and prayed that things would change for me.

Two years later, at the age of 13, I transferred to Culler Middle School in Lincoln, Nebraska. I loved my school; I had many friends and people who did not bullying me and I just loved my life. My mom wasn't depressed anymore and my now three siblings and I were living an awesome life. Everything seemed to be going good and then my mom decided she wanted to move to Georgia. I was shocked and hurt when my mom told me we were moving to Georgia. I was super bummed which caused me to fall back into depression. When we first moved to Georgia, we stayed in hotels until my mom got approved for our place. I recall the entire time my mom kept saying that we cannot lose faith. I did not understand, nor did I care about that; I just wanted to go back to Lincoln. My mother was upset, and I told her we had made the wrong decision by moving there, but she did not listen. Shortly afterwards, we found our place and moved into some apartments. While living there, we had some issues with bugs and my mom was ready to move again. It was a depressing stay.

One day, my brother Jordan and I went outside to play with the other kids we were trying to fit in with. My brother decided to pull the fire alarm which caused everyone to evacuate out of their apartments. We pretended that we didn't know what happened, but my mom knew. She said she felt it in her gut that me and my brother were the culprits. The police and fire department were everywhere, and it was a disaster. Very upset, my mom told us we were going to move with are aunt in Omaha, Nebraska because she was tired of us disrespecting her. I was very sad knowing that I would never be able to see my mom or other siblings again.

Moving to Omaha was the worst three months of my life. We were yelled at, accused of doing things that we didn't do and even physically abused. I couldn't call to tell my mom because I felt like she wouldn't care since she was disappointed with us. My brother finally called and begged my mom to please come rescue us and she came immediately. When she arrived, she had the biggest smile on her face. Seeing our mom pull up in the driveway to pick us up was amazing! It gave me this joy that I cannot explain; you just have to had experienced it to know what I am talking about. I realized at that moment just how much I loved and appreciated her. When we got back to Georgia, we were still living in the same apartment, but I was happy and I didn't care.

A couple days later, there was a shooting outside of our home. When we saw the person shooting and running, it scared us. My mom had us all to get down onto the floor and crawl into our rooms. Later that night we found out that the guy died right outside our window and our home was taped up as a crime scene. My mom stopped at nothing to get us out of that apartment. We moved a couple weeks later into a big house. It was one of the houses that my mom had been riding by and praying. She would say, "I claim it in Jesus' name!"

I never understood why she would do that or have me and my siblings pile up in the car to ride through neighborhoods with huge houses just to look and pray on the way back to our apartment that she would get one. After moving in this home, it all began to make sense to me. I began to finally understand why my mom went through what she went through and why she moved us to. I then understood why she always would talk about obedience and faith. Now we have many good friends, unconditional love and things are getting brighter each day around the house and in our lives. Currently, I am being homeschooled and working with Dr. Ellison and Men Magnifying Manhood Movement. I love my life and I don't want to change any part of it. The bad parts of my life prepared me for these good parts. My mom says it is what helps build my substance and one day I will be able to pour back into young boys. When I get older, I want to go to the Marines, have a beautiful family, be a minister, move to New York and help kids who have been through something that I've been through. I am striving to live my life by God's will and not my own. Thank you for reading my story and my testimony!

~Dedication~

This is dedicated to my mother, Sadie Evans who always believed in me. To my siblings Jordan, Lorenzo, Langston and Amira, thank you guys for loving me. To Dr. Ellison, my mentor and the Men Magnifying Manhood Movement, thank you for giving me a chance. To my grandpa, Steve Betts, thank you for always picking up my calls and loving me. Finally and most importantly to God for giving me life and health.

Biography of Bishop H. Vonzell Castilla

Bishop H. Vonzell Castilla was born in Madison County, Mississippi, the seventh child of Willenham and Theresa Castilla. Because he was the seventh child, older relatives regaled him with folklore and superstition about the special powers and discernment he would receive. *He's still waiting.*

Hilliard V. Castilla attended Christ Missionary & Industrial High School (C.M.&.I) until 1978 when he was accepted for early admission to Jackson State University. After graduating with honors in 1978, Bishop Castilla attended the University Of Virginia School Of Law where he received his *Juris Doctorate* in 1982. Upon graduation, Bishop Castilla was honored to serve as a judicial clerk for the Honorable Joseph Hatchett, United Sates Court of Appeals for the Eleventh Circuit. He is licensed to practice law in Mississippi and Georgia and is a partner in the law firm of Waldon, Adelman, Castilla, Hiestand & Prout.

In 2000, Bishop Castilla was appointed to the Committee on Children and the Courts by the State Bar of Georgia. His *pro bono* work includes serving as Attorney and *Guardian Ad Litem* for Georgia's highly successful Truancy Intervention Project.

Bishop Castilla presently serves as pastor of Higher Calling Ministries, Church of Christ (Holiness) U.S.A. (COCHUSA) in Decatur, Georgia. Consecrated to the bishopric in 2016, Bishop

Castilla also serves as presiding prelate of the Southeastern Diocese of COCHUSA. Prior to this elevation, Bishop Castilla served as President of the National Sunday School & Holiness Youth Ministries of COCHUSA. Bishop Castilla has also served on numerous boards, including Wheaton College Board of Visitors, Beulah Urban Outreach and DOOR Atlanta, a nationally renowned organization which provides service opportunities for young people. Hilliard has been recognized by the State Bar of Georgia and other organizations for mentoring young people and challenging others to serve.

Bishop Castilla has written numerous plays, skits and youth ministry aids. In 2016 he published his first book, *Make God Look Good*.

Hilliard V. Castilla is married to the lovely and gracious Tiffany C. Castilla. They have three awesome children: Amira, Kendall and Lydia.

Personal Profile

Key Words
Service, Faithfulness, Vision, Leadership, Courage, Triumph

Favorite Quotes
Brethren, I count not myself to have apprehended: but this one thing I do, forgetting those things which are behind, and reaching forth unto those things which are before, I press toward the mark for the prize of the high calling of God in Christ Jesus.
(Philippians 3:13-14)

Values
Christ-centeredness, Family, Integrity, Gratitude, Respect, Pursuit of Justice

Marketable Skills
Leadership Training, Writing, Conflict Resolution, Creative Thinking, Vision Casting, Critical Analysis

Contact Information
Email: hcastilla@aol.com
LinkedIn: Hilliard Castilla

Vonzell Castilla

WORDS OF WISDOM

Reflections on the Importance of Sage Advice, Passed Down

Bishop H. Vonzell Castilla

*W*e are family, I got all my sisters with me; we are family, get up everybody and sing!" The disco anthem by Sister Sledge blared through the loudspeakers at Three Rivers Stadium in Pittsburgh, Pennsylvania where I spent a summer for a quantitative skills institute at Carnegie Mellon University. Going over to the stadium to watch my favorite baseball team was a welcome respite from the grueling routine of studying, attending classes and completing homework, a schedule that some of my brainy classmates seemed to relish. Not me. I needed to get away every now and then, and there was no better place to spend summer nights than Three Rivers Stadium, where I could see my beloved Pirates, known then as "the Lumber Company," demolish various interlopers who came to town.

In addition to watching my favorite team play ball at a championship level, I also reveled in the sense of togetherness displayed by the

37

"Bucs" (another name for the team). They were truly a baseball family. On the field they performed like a well-oiled machine. The outfielders always hit the cutoff man; sluggers didn't mind opting for the sacrifice fly and bunting to move a man over was celebrated. Likewise, a sense of unity prevailed in the clubhouse. Even the casual observer could see the comradery. They laughed together, offered constructive criticism and generally displayed an "all for one, one for all" attitude. I believe it was this commitment to unity, as much as athletic prowess and managerial expertise (both of which they had in abundance) which led to the team's overall success, including a World Series victory in 1979.

Reminiscing about the Pirates and their unity invariably takes me back even further; way, way back to Jackson, Mississippi, outside the county line where I grew up. I remember growing up in a community where people genuinely cared for one another; where they looked out for one another, protected one another and challenged one another. This was a place where you felt the neighbor across the street desired to push you along, not hold you back. A place where the family across the field celebrated when you achieved and grieved when you didn't. A place called . . . home. The longer I live, the more I realize that it was not only my immediate family, but also the collective values and wisdom of our community which helped to propel me to whatever level of success I have achieved. Here is some of that wisdom:

<u>LISTEN TO OTHERS</u>

It has been said that we have two ears and one mouth for a reason: we need to talk less and listen more. This wisdom was dispensed by my father and reinforced by other family members, parishioners, neighbors and teachers. They collectively frowned upon those who talked more than they listened. One of the most popular nuggets of wisdom regularly dispensed was this gem: "An empty wagon makes a lot of noise." Yes, I know this proverb seems quaint and old fashioned now, but it is, in reality, more relevant than ever; for we now live in times where style is elevated over substance, where talking a good game is more important that doing what's required and where turning up the volume is more important than veracity. We desperately need people, especially young people, in our communities who have the wisdom to listen. Yes, it's true that experience is a great teacher, but too many make life altering mistakes that they could have avoided by simply listening to someone. (Proverbs 12:15)

Here's an example of how the simple act of listening changed the course of my life. Growing up in rural Mississippi, I, like most of my peers, dreamed of playing professional sports. I loved all the major sports but spent most of my dream time on basketball. It seems that every night I saw myself bringing the ball up the court for the Los Angeles Lakers, side by side with *The Logo* Jerry West (back then he was known as "Mr. Clutch"). I was a good scorer in high school - averaging 22 points per game -- and went by the nickname "Von the Gun." I vividly remember the chants from my classmates when I went on a scoring tear; they would say, "Von the Gun, Number 1!" Nobody could tell me back then that I wasn't going to the NBA and start at point guard for the Lakers. Nobody, but Kathy, that is. Kathy is my sister-in-law and back then she worked as a teacher at my school, Christ Missionary and Industrial College (C.M. & I). One day she asked me what I wanted to do once I graduated. I told her proudly that I was going to play college and then professional basketball. Kathy looked at me with a mixture of curiosity, concern and compassion before uttering the simple words that changed my direction: "Von," she said, "Why don't you use your mind?" She went on to offer that I had a good mind and should endeavor to use it. Because Kathy and I have always been close, I listened and took her words to heart. As I meditated on her counsel, it occurred to me that she was probably right. I averaged 22 points per game, but I played for a small private school against questionable competition. I was only 5" 10" tall and was not a great leaper; neither was I exceptionally fast or strong. I could shoot the ball, but (during those days) shooters were a dime a dozen. Yes, I received a little acclaim at school, but no one scouted or recruited me. The more I thought about it, the more Kathy's words ("Why don't you use your mind?") made sense to me. I soon set aside my obsession with basketball and concentrated on the ACT exam. I scored well enough to gain early admission to Jackson State University and went from there to the University of Virginia Law School. I thank God that Kathy took the time to talk to me and that I had the sense to listen.

LIFT UP YOUR HEAD

Where I come from you were not allowed to look down when speaking; neither were you allowed to sulk when things didn't go your way. The unspoken community mantra was "look up"; the spoken out loud – and I mean loud – command from my grandmother was "boy, hold your head up!" Magolia "Gold Baby" Castilla was the epitome of the strong, supportive black grandmother who helped our communities to survive and thrive. She was an encourager par excellence but was not afraid to confront and challenge as she helped to usher young people into adulthood. But my grandmother had a special burden -- an oft cited concern -- for the well-being of "black boys." She was determined to "push black boys because they grow into the men who must lead" families and churches. She was also well-aware of the vicious assault upon black males by the larger society. So, she encouraged, and pushed, and encouraged, and pushed, and encouraged…you get the idea. If you came into her presence looking down or acting timid, she would chastise you severely: "Boy, what's wrong with you? Lift up your head." We need more Magolia Castilla's today; those willing to encourage and challenge our young people to hold their heads up high – regardless of the circumstances.

I can't say it with the earth-shattering intensity of my grandmother, but I can express the same sentiment. Lift up your head. Don't consider yourself to be less than anybody else, regardless of your station in life. We are all created in God's image; therefore, He has deposited something in each of us worth redeeming, worth building on, worth … His ultimate sacrifice. So, if you don't have the ideal family background, lift up your head, you're created in God's image and He wants what's best for you. Trust in the Lord and keep striving, keep pushing, keep going until God takes you where you're destined to be. Lift up your head, even if you get knocked down; for if you can look up, you can get up. If you can get up, you can get back in the fight, and if you stay in the fight long enough, you'll win! (1 John 4:4)

LEAD BY EXAMPLE

"Be a leader, not a follower." It's a statement my kids, mentees, church members and others have heard me utter on numerous occasions. But here's a confession: it's not original. I lifted this gem from my father Willenham Castilla who used to say it when he served as Sunday school superintendent at New Lake Church of Christ (Holiness) U.S.A. in Jackson, Mississippi. He made the statement, but he wasn't the only one who expressed the sentiment. It was stated, implied, suggested and modeled by countless adults who took an interest in guiding me and other young people in the

41

right direction. It has proven to be some of the most sage and useful advice I've ever received. Why?

First, this advice encourages you to develop and follow your own viewpoints as opposed to mindlessly following in the footsteps of others. We all have something to offer. Sadly, we never get to consider the viewpoints of many because they are afraid to chart their own way, preferring instead to simply follow others. Leadership development allows for a more interesting, diverse and rewarding marketplace of ideas, something sorely needed in our communities. Let's preach: "Be a leader, not a follower."

Second, the encouragement to lead (as opposed to blindly following) helps to prevent some from engaging in harmful, socially deviant behaviors. Those who blindly follow can be led to do almost anything, even to the point of engaging in foolish criminal acts. I speak from experience. When I worked in juvenile court, I saw hundreds of young men who got caught up in the criminal justice system as the result of following someone's foolish lead. Some knucklehead would suggest breaking in a store in broad daylight and the follower would just go along without thinking of the absurdity of the enterprise, or the consequences of getting caught. Those who are taught to think for themselves ask the right questions (especially about consequences) and make wise decisions. Let's teach: "Be a leader, not a follower." (1 Timothy 4:12)

Finally, the encouragement to chart one's own course helps to develop the bold, visionary leadership qualities our communities, nation and world so desperately need. When you think about it, our greatest leaders were those who went against the conventional wisdom of their day. Fredrick Douglas refused to accept the prevailing sentiment of his time regarding slavery, choosing instead to push for abolition of the brutal, inhumane institution while declaring "without friction, there is no progress." Likewise, the Rev. Dr. Martin Luther King refused to follow the "give it time" mantra of his day regarding segregation, pushing instead for its demise while explaining *"Why We Can't Wait."* Many told President Barack Obama that he was crazy to spend his time and resources running for the nation's highest office. Thank God he had the *Audacity of Hope* and chose to be a leader and not just a follower.

When I reflect on my time rooting for the Pirates, my mind invariably centers on Willie Stargell, the Hall of Famer known as much for his leadership and affable manner as for his tape measure home runs. The other players would always gather around Stargell, waiting for him to dispense some nugget of wisdom; and Stargell, known as "Pops" later in his career, would always oblige. When asked the key to his success Stargell stated, "I'm a God-fearing man who worship with my heart and my life." How profound. Though he won a Most Valuable Player Award, two World Series and countless other awards, Stargell attributed his success to worshiping the Lord. The upshot? Listening, lifting (your head) and leading are admirable traits, but these attributes, like any others, can only be fully realized, can only lead to true success when embodied in someone like Stargell – or you -- who dares to worship the Lord with his life.

~Dedication~

Judah Allen, GA

Jermaine Allen, GA

Josh Bissoon, GA

Kayden Burkhalter, GA

Sammie Burkhalter, GA

Andy Bissoon-Wright, GA

Ahmad Campbell, GA

Kendall Castilla, GA

Terrance Fountain, GA

Terrell Fountain, GA

Alex Greene, GA

Joshua Key, GA

Amari Paige, GA

Isaiah Rayburn, GA

Grant Smith, GA

Miles Smith, GA

Artis Tucker, Jr.

Elijah Williams, GA

Michael Wilson, GA

Jakiah Wright, GA

Biography of Bishop Samie L. Conyers

Bishop Samie L. Conyers was born in Miami, Florida, October 3, 1955, to the parents of Mr. Sam Conyers Sr. and Mrs. Rachel Fulton. He grew up without a father in the home, and had one brother, Alvin Fulton, two sisters Sarah Conyers-Collin and Vebaly Ann Howard-Brown. His mother had one more daughter in later years, Wenona Whyte. Bishop Conyers found out many years later that his father had another baby boy from another woman, and his name was Otis Reed. Bishop Samie Conyers graduated from Miami Central High in June 1974, received an Associate in General Studies from Central Texas College, Associate of Art from Frederick Community College, and Bachelor of Art Degree in Counseling from American College of Theology. He graduated from The Leadership Institute, Grassroots Activist School, and obtained membership with African-American Community College Trustees Association (ACCT). Pastor Conyers joined the United States Army in June of 1975, as Communication Specialist, and retired after 23 years as a Sergeant First Class E-7. He worked as a Platoon Sergeant, Company Equal-Opportunity Non-Commission Officer Representative for over nine years, Community Civil/ Human Rights leader in Germany and in South Korea, a USA Army Unit Master Physical Fitness Trainer. He retired in November 1998, from the 1110th Signal Battalion, Autodin Switching Center Manager at Ft. Detrick, Maryland in the grade of Sergeant First Class. SFC Conyers was also elected as the

45

Fort Derick Joint Armed Forces President representing over 300,000 retirees and Active Duty service members in that area of Maryland.

He is happily married to his high school sweetheart Mrs. Brenda (Humes) Conyers, daughter of Mr. Link and Mrs. Naomi Humes. They celebrated 43 short years of a happy and blessed marriage, and over 40 years in ministry. They have one daughter, Senitta Conyers, a current graduate of Florida Memorial University in Miami, Florida, but living in Frederick, Maryland.

Bishop and First Lady Brenda Conyers has over 40 years of pastoral experience. The Conyers family started home missionary works in West Germany, Taegu, South Korea and Pusan. Bishop Conyers was the Senior Pastor and founder of Grace Pentecostal Worship Center Inc., in Frederick Maryland for 11 years. Presently pastoring at Calvary New Life Tabernacle in Decatur, Georgia, Bishop Conyers, with Elder Winn and others conduct a Calvary's Boys-to-Men Mentorship program in DeKalb County. Pastor Samie and Sister Brenda Conyers started their missionary ministry from Ft. Rile, Kansas in 1976, reaching the Gulley Family, who are now in ministry in Alba. After one year, the US Army transferred Bishop Conyers from Kansas to Ludwigsburg/ Stuttgart Germany community for three years of tour of duty. This was the beginning of their first of four missionary journeys overseas. Upon returning to the States, he was ordained under the United Pentecostal Church International, in 1982 while stationed at Ft. Sheridan in Illinois, and started a church on Ft. Sheridan Army base outside Chicago, Illinois. He was consecrated as an Ordained Bishop with Apostolic Ministries Inc. by Bishop Alvin McCoy in November, 2005. Also in the public service arena during his 14 years in Maryland, Bishop Conyers was a candidate for Frederick County State Representative, Frederick County Commissioner, Frederick County School Board member, and City of Frederick Alderman.

All of his experience in life from childhood in Coconut Grove on the other side of the railroad tracks, later moved to Liberty City, Florida and on to Miami's central area, and around the world in the U.S. Army, helped him to grow up, develop and become a man "magnifying manhood" to the glory of God, and as a community servant leader, building men for ministry!

Personal Profile

Key Phrases to Live By
- Faith, belief in God, service to others.
- Help somebody each day, that my life and living won't be in vain!
- Don't sweat the small stuff. It's going to get better.
- If I can help somebody each day, to God be the glory!

Favorite Quotes
- If it is to be, it's up to me.
- I am my brother's keeper.
- Ask not what your country can do for you, but what can I do for God's glory in my country?

Values
Dignity, Respect, Intensity, Country, Family, Moral, Caring, Compassion, Dedication, Belief in Others and God-fearing

Marketable Skills

County Civil and Human Rights Commissioner, Communication Specialist, Signal School Instructor/Writer, Equal-Opportunity Instructor, Non- commission Officer, US Army Master Fitness Trainer certified, Management, building people for their full potential, Public Speaking, Leading Group leadership to success, Networking, Mentoring & Developing young men for manhood

Contact Information

Address: 4321 Pasuth Lane, Conley, GA 30288
Email: souls4theking@aol.com
Facebook: Bishopsamieconyers
Telephone: 404-675-9293

THE IMPORTANCE OF MENTORSHIP AND HIGHER EDUCATION

Bishop Samie L. Conyers

We have learned to watch, pray, listen, learn, grow and receive change, by the important values of mentorship in men magnifying manhood throughout our lives. I am a compassionate community activist originally from Miami, Florida. I lived in Frederick, Maryland area for 14 years, three years before I retired from the military in November, 1998. I was blessed to have traveled around the nation, championing educational equity for minorities in the Frederick County school system and on the campus of Frederick Community College, as a Frederick Community College Board of Trustee member, appointed by former Gov. Robert L. Ehrich, of the State of Maryland.

I developed the existing men's ministry in keeping with church purpose and direction; equipping men to be god-fearing leaders and effective disciples, husbands, and fathers. At Calvary New Life Tabernacle Church in Atlanta Ga., our objectives of Men's ministry are to disciple and equip the boys, who are becoming young men with a clear understanding of their roles as men of God magnifying

49

manhood, whether they are single, married, young or older. We all have room for improvement, and growth. Living isolated from active fellowship of other men is not an option. No man is an island by themselves. We all need someone to learn from and teach us the right things to do.

Proverb 27:17 - *"Iron sharpens iron, so one man sharpens another man."* The principle here is men need encouragement, mentorship training, fellowship, and real role models who can magnify manhood, across our nation, to perform great things for the glory of God!

In the book of Genesis, God created mankind in His own image. God created Adam the first man from the dust of the ground and breath into the nostrils of man the breath of life (Genesis 1:26-27; 2:7). Therefore, men were created in the image of God, to listen, learn, grow, change and obey the voice of God. As a man, we must seek to please and magnify the glory of God, as we grow into manhood. *"God said, 'Let us make man in our image, according to our likeness; let them have dominion over the fish of the sea, over the birds of the air, and over the cattle, over all the earth"* (Genesis 1:26).

We learned that the Word became flesh. Jesus Christ was God, made in the image of a mankind. This is one of the greatest revelations made known to mankind, by God! In John 1:14, it states *"And the Word became flesh and dwelt among us, and we have seen his glory, glory as of the only Son from the Father, full of grace and truth.* O' praise God for this indescribable bible truth revealed to man.

There are some natural, spiritual and physical qualities in godly men magnifying manhood. I am a leader who demonstrates traits of a man magnifying manhood and coming into the fullness of spiritual and natural maturity; a spiritual leader committed to the cause of teaching Jesus Christ to other young men in their communities. A leader must be a guide at home and in the local community embracing the covenant of life from boyhood to manhood. A great leader should pattern his life after Christ, be a true worshipper, and lead by example, teaching young men how to have a healthy marriage and family life.

From a child to manhood, I wanted to be brave son, loving, firmly built, who loved all his family members, patriotic, caring about his friends, neighbors and community. The old television movie "Combat" influenced me a lot, by helping me to understand that war was a fight for freedom and the country you lived in. It was an honor to serve as a U.S. Army soldier, defender of God and country. I wanted to be physically strong, mentally tough, robust, healthy, strong in the faith, with a spirit of self-sacrifice, honoring God, his family & country. I was determined to live by the words of the late President John F. Kennedy, "Ask not what your country can do for you, but what can you do for your country?"

My father was Missing in Action (MIA). Since my father did not live with us, he did not play an important part in my life. As noted in the military, he was missing in action (MIA). My sister Sarah and I only visited him a few times a month, if that much. My other sister Ann Howard would visit her father also, who lived in the Miami area, next door to the world renowned Cassius Clay, before he became a Muslim in 1961, changing his name to Muhammad Ali and winning the World Heavyweight Championship from Sonny Liston. I missed growing up with my older brother Alvin Fulton, because he was sent to my grandmother Francis Fulton, to ease the load on my mother. She worked two jobs at a time, to pay the bills and put food on our table. My two uncles Roosevelt and Lee Fulton were around often to give some guidance. I remember my sisters and I going fishing with them. My favorite Aunt Sarah Dawson was our family enforcer, when my mother was at work, sick, or not at home.

I was a small, skinny boy, bullied by others at school. I had trouble reading, and bout with physical sickness as a child, continually going in and out of the hospital. At one point in the first grade, I had double pneumonia infections in both lungs. I was not expected to live, so all my family members came to the hospital to visit me. I remember lying in the hospital bed with a big clear tent looming over the entire bed. Back in the 1960's, double pneumonia was common but I remained in the hospital for a long time. Unable to attend school much that year, I had to repeat first grade. But, God had a plan and purpose for my life (Jeremiah 29:11). Thank God, I survived! Another time as a child I remember playing with an old red rocking chair in our home. A nail was sticking out of the corner of it, and I, not knowing the danger, kept rocking it. Finally, it hit me, above my right eyebrow. Bleeding badly, I was taken to the local hospital. I survived and have a scar today as a reminder. Another memory of how God kept me was when someone and I were playing in the closet with matches, setting my grandmother's house on fire. Yet again, I survived! We made it out okay, but, I still remember the spanking I received. I learned many valuable lesson in life, while growing up without a father in our home. My mother called me her problem child because I was full of energy and always getting into something.

We lived in the Coconut Grove Projects, a poor community, then moved to another low-income housing project called Peyton Place in the Brownville community of Miami, Florida. However, we were not aware that it was a low income housing project. Our neighborhood always had something going on, good and bad. We were young teenagers, some were a part of a so-called gangs, parents had fights all the time, young boys were stealing from the corner store, getting into trouble in the community. There were groups of older gang members, shooting at each other and running from the local police. I had many friends, Bobby and Vernon Pascal family, the Fletcher's three boys, and my neighborhood school mate, Ronald Robinson, who had a large family. They were very poor and he was bad company for me, because as teenagers, we stayed in trouble. I started early to earn since I learned the need for money. I became a newspaper boy for the Miami Herald and my mother bought me a bicycle to ride on my little newspaper route. She also signed me up for Cub Scouts and I joined the Club Scouts of America in Dade County, while she became our Den Mother Leader. My mother tried to keep me active and out of trouble by playing football in the Miami Optimist League in the sixth and seventh grade. Mr. Ernest Mills or Miller was our coach; he was a tough coach, but not a bad person.

In 1974, I graduated from Miami Central High School. During the summer, I worked at the Alcoa Park swimming pool for four years. We taught smaller children in grade school how to swim. In the fall, I attended Florida Memorial University for one year; then I joined the U.S. Army on May 28, 1975. This was my first major trip out of Miami, Florida, to Basic Training Station at Fort Jackson, South Carolina. Eventually, I would travel around the world at our government's expense. Exposed to a whole new lifestyle and adventures, I was blessed to meet many other men who helped develop my character and made me the person I am, today; an older and wiser man magnifying manhood to the glory of God.

Now the rest of my life, I have dedicated to building good character in boys who will become young men and young men who will become good citizen and community leaders in the future.

While growing up in the rough community projects, one day one of my friends asked me, why was I so kind, free-hearted, friendly, sharing my things with others, and always defending others? I told them that my mother and family always taught us to do right, and treat everybody fairly. Remember the "Golden Rule…" *Do unto others, as you would like someone to do unto you!*

Vernon Pascal told me, "You probably will become a lawyer someday, defending people!"

By the grace of God, I have held many professions and titles in the United States Army and as a civilian, but most importantly, I became a converted disciple of Jesus Christ. Jesus said, "Follow me, and I will make you fishers of men" (Matthew 4:19).

"If anyone would come after me, let him deny himself, take up his cross daily, and follow me" (Luke 9:23). Often, the path God wants for us leads a different direction from the one we or our friends would choose. It's the choice between the broad way and the narrow way (Matthew 7:13). Jesus knows the purpose for which He created us. Discovering that purpose and living it is the secret to real happiness.

Early in life, I tried to find real joy, peace, happiness, and a good relationship with other women, and people in my life. We know that everyone wants to be loved by somebody, and have hope to find a partner for life. At some point, I noticed an emptiness and void in my heart. Something was missing and it could only be filled by God's Spirit! Man-made religion, education, human philosophy, wealth, nor material gain from this world, can satisfy that longing in your soul. Only Jesus can satisfy your soul. After I was married to my high school sweetheart Brenda Humes, the military transferred me to Fort Riley, Kansas. It was there in Junction City, Kansas, we were invited to Faith Tabernacle, UPC church, by Sgt. Gerald Harris and SPC Archie Matthews. My wife and I started attending church regularly, was filled with the Holy Spirit, and forever changed by the presence of the Lord.

Now, I am a man on a mission with a calling to serve the people of my communities. To magnify manhood, I believe we must always strive to do something good in the city for others. Whether it is fighting to stop gun violence, illegal drugs, gang killings, crimes, and the injustices towards our black males in our prison system, we must do something. How about we start trying to keep young black men in school and out of jail? There was over 800,000 black men in prison back then. Currently today, there are 2.3 million black men in jail or prison in the United States of America! There about 64 percent of black homes with women and children living alone. More prevalent than ever, black men are missing in action (MIA), and we wonder what's going on? That's a big problem, an epidemic problem. We must face the facts, and try to fix the problems in our communities by starting with us. Are we really men magnifying manhood or are we magnifying ourselves?

~Dedication~

Mrs. Rachel Whyte-Fulton, Miami, FL

Brenda Conyers, Atlanta, GA

Deaconess Sarah Conyers-Collie

Alvin Fulton, Palm Bay, FL

Vebaly Ann Howard, Atlanta, GA

Bishop and Mrs. Fred Moutrie, Pensacola, FL

Bishop Alvin McCoy, Pennsylvania

Rev. Samuel Graham, Sumter. SC

Pastor Wilbert and Sis Glen Blandon

Pastor Roderick Jackson, Leesville, LA

Pastor Michael Williams, Alaska

Bishop Robert (Bobby) Stewart, Miami, FL

*Former Military Fellowship Missionary,
Pastor Reverend Artie Enis*

Late Pastor Reverend Wayne Rooks

Late Elder Gerald Harris

Late Missionary Dale Starks

Late Wilfred Brewster

Late Bishop Leonard Westberg

To God be all the glory!

Biography of Jamal Davis

 **Jamal Davis**, is a husband, entrepreneur and youth leader. He is a new business owner, leading an application developing company. Serving as youth president for five years, Jamal invests and pours out into the lives of youth and young adults. He has served as the President of Impact, a small group at Georgia State University that tasks itself with positively impacting the community. Jamal and his wife have been married for five years.

Personal Profile

Key Words
Phenomenal, Amazing, Spectacular

Favorite Quote
"He who takes no risks achieves nothing."

Values
Establishing Strong Relationships, Networking, Encouraging Others, Being Effective

Marketable Skills
Public Speaking, Leading, Networking

Contact Information
Email: jhdavis116@gmail.com
LinkedIn.com: Jamal Davis
Facebook: https://www.facebook.com/jamalhdavis

FINDING YOUR IMAGE

Jamal Davis

I was born and raised in the rough neighborhood of Paterson, New Jersey that was overshadowed by gangs, violence, and mischief. My parents split shortly after having me and from as early as I can remember, my mother started dating and was married in no time. During this time, I remember being happy to have another male figure in my life although I really loved my father. I didn't realize that the reason for this was because of the newly developing void in my life. My father was around, but not present. He did not play the role of a father or show me how to be a man. I would remember countless times asking him if I could stay the weekend with him, which he agreed to. However, he never showed or gave an explanation of why he was absent. This caused me to attempt to cling to my stepfather; however instead of finding solace and affirmation, I was met with abuse and hate.

Surprisingly, I never saw how damaging these experiences were. I just brushed them under the rug and never addressed it. Most male children tend to emulate and follow their father's example. There is a sense of completion and fulfillment when you can connect with and make your father feel proud. This is what I wanted and never experienced. My father was a workaholic and was very promiscuous. Having that exposure so early to transient sexual relationships opened a door to sexual strongholds in my life.

With this sexual exposure and interest, at a tender age of seven, I allowed myself to be taken advantage of and was molested by a friend of the family. He had a way with words and manipulated me. He forced me to remain silent and this abuse lasted seven years. I did not reveal this to my mother until I was 21, only months away from getting married. This opened up my sexual appetite and I found myself inappropriately touching women and wanting to gratify my lusts. Operating like this made me realize that I did not have any respect for women and failed to understand their worth. Defective and wounded, I followed in the footsteps of my lustful father.

Today's trend and unspoken rule in the environment of men are that if a lady passes by, we must look. Once she has passed by, depending on what we see, we should make the decision whether or not we make a sexual pursuit. A lot of men don't understand the value of women. Over the years many cultures, religions and political systems have devalued women. The expression of women inferiority to men and their usefulness has impacted the scope of women rights. Most men believe that women are beneath them and only good in the kitchen or bedroom. This way of thinking only makes us miss the value in women.

Prior to getting married, I dated for a great portion of my life. I always trusted myself to find the best woman possible. But that did not work out so well as my only criteria for finding one was based on appearance. I never thought to look for more defining characteristics such as, if she was a woman of virtue or did she know her worth. When I found my wife, she was not only beautiful but virtuous and strong. She was confident and knew her worth. She had an undying love and passion for God and was ready to allow me to lead her. I thank God for her and I am truly blessed to have found someone who compliments me so well and supports me like no other. I am also thankful to have built spiritual principles that help guide me to see the value in women so I *could* find my wife.

As a man, I learned that we must always acknowledge the worth of a woman by showing her respect and investing time in building her up. Our society today devalues women and makes it seem as if they are insignificant and less important than men. I believe a woman is just as important as a man because if not, God would not found it fit to give a man a helpmate. Without women, it would be impossible to fulfill the will of God.

As men, we should magnify our manhood by respecting and valuing the women in our lives. In this process, we would positively impact our community and provide the right example for young men to follow. This example will help teach young men to love and honor women rather than treat them as a materialistic object. This will help many young children avoid growing up in a broken family and avoid the neglect of the missing parent. There are cases where a family can be broken but the parents can co-exist and support one another. This is what we must strive towards.

As I reflect I realize that having the wrong male influence in my life made things take a turn for the worse. My sex-driven father made me not see the value in women. Likewise, my abusive stepfather also had a strong impact, as I found myself emulating his aggressiveness and verbal abuse. I also developed an untamed temper. It felt good to treat women harshly and to argue and harass them. I gave my mother hell growing up and that anger translated into other relationships. It was so horrible that I was required by my school to attend counseling sessions. By this time, my mother divorced her husband because of unfaithfulness and the way he treated me. With no male figure in the house and no help from my father, my mother panicked. She believed that the lifestyle I was living, and the friends I was involved with, would ultimately lead to my demise. She factored in the statistical possibility of me getting involved with gangs in my neighborhood, so she knew she had to make a move.

After thinking critically and praying hard, she decided that it would be best if we moved out of the environment. So, at the age of eleven, we moved to Atlanta, Georgia, where my mother believed we would have a fresh start. Sometimes it is beneficial to change your environment because your surroundings have a direct impact on your lifestyle. The Bible states that bad company corrupts good character (1 Corinthians 15:33, NIV). If you mingle with someone who has a problem stealing, you will probably find yourself pressured to do the same, even if it is not a desire you have. As men, we should seek to connect only with people who share the same passions of ambition and success; men or women who can invest, mentor, and motivate us to get to our finish line. We should separate ourselves from individuals who are negative and cannot effectively contribute to our lives.

Once I arrived in Georgia, I instantly attempted to fit in. I tried to look the part and walk the part but I only ended up being bullied. I did not know how to fight, reason or operate as a young man. The only life lessons I could draw from were those from my mother. No matter how great of a parent she was, she could never be my father and could not teach me how to be a man. I was bullied and abused so much that I struggled with rejection. I felt like I had no significance and was not appreciated or loved. Up until that point, my father had never said he was proud of me or made one recognizable sacrifice for me. In fact, all I could remember of him was the times he stood me up. Most of the times, when I actually stayed with him, he was never there. He mostly left me with my stepmother while he traveled. I lacked confidence and strength and found myself plunging deeper into trouble.

In a desperate attempt to feel significant, I joined a gang at my school. I wanted the young men in this gang to respect and appreciate me. They did to some extent but I found myself caught up in something that made me make horrible decisions and not too long after, I wanted out. All that I lacked as a child brought me to a low point in my life that I never believed that I could come back from. A few years later, my mother lost her house and things got worse.

Rejection is prevalent in the lives of many men. The absence of a father does significant damage and can cause men to form broken relationships. Most times men do not have any examples to look to in becoming a man and have to rely on media and entertainment, which portrays false images of manhood. In order to deal with rejection, you must first confront it and allow God to heal you as you forgive those who contributed to it.

Aware of my needs, my mother stepped up and tried to help develop masculine traits within me. She desired me to be a lot more responsible. At the age of sixteen, she required me to pay rent. I heavily opposed this decision but to no avail. I failed to see that God was trying to break cycles in my life and wanted to develop me into a man. As I struggled to find manhood, I was able to find reprieve. I broke free from the intimate lifestyle that I struggled with through the grace and power of God. I found Christ at a testimonial baptism service and since then, my entire life took a different turn.

I attended a deliverance ministry which changed my whole outlook on life and God. My church served as the catalyst that helped me break through years of oppression. I developed confidence, morality, and a heart of forgiveness. Before I attended this church, I did not think freedom was possible and I saw religion as more of an avenue for entertainment and theatrics, not power and change. I was able to stop inappropriately touching women and I found the strength to confront the individual who molested me and forgive him. I now see that a lot of the pain and damage done in the past can only be healed by God and one must go through the necessary process to address the situations. I realized that no matter how strong I was or how hard I tried, I could never get to where I needed to be in life by myself. God is all-powerful and gracious to help us break the addictions we have and strengthen our weaknesses.

Even though I had spiritual enlightenment, I still found myself struggling with rejection. I did not know how to talk to men or be around them nor how to fit in with people. I tried so hard to get into relationships so that I could have someone love and respect me. I thought that an imperfect human being could complete me and I was so wrong. As determined as I was to please my significant other, expecting to receive the same in return, it was never enough. Another person cannot fix the years of hurt and pain you have dealt with. Only God can fill that void while walking you through the healing process. Many times, we make that mistake and look for remedies in the wrong places, which could lead to our demise.

As I reflect, I remembered struggling to do things well because I did not have an active father who could invest time into developing my manhood. I did not know how to talk to a girl, or how to play basketball. I did not even know how to dress properly. I could not find my identity and I found that I was emulating too much from my mother. So much so that I had certain feminine traits that I despised. As I continued to faithfully attend my ministry, I started to realize that the more invested I was in God, the more I started to develop skills, talents, and gifts. The first gift I found was that I loved to write and was somewhat decent. The second was that although I used to be a shy unconfident person, my confidence had soared and I was really good at public speaking.

Another trait that I developed was patience, which took my mother by surprise. Almost my entire childhood, I had an aggressive attitude, always talking back and getting into fights. Through the power of God, I was able to remain humble and calm. God was healing me from the pain of my past and filling me with positive traits. As we submit to God, He sheds light on the many talents and gifts that He places on the inside. He then causes them to grow and be nurtured so He can use them. When God uses your gifts and talents, they bring forth the most success that you will ever experience. Being a man of faith is necessary for all men because it allows you to be fully capable of leading a family.

As God continued to move, He positioned a spiritual leader, father, and mentor into my life. The pastor of my church pushed it back on track. Throughout this whole process, I learned that in order to grow and develop, you need a mentor in your life. My pastor was that for me and more. He went beyond the call of duty as a pastor and he adopted me as his own son and taught me things my father never did. I learned how to talk to women, how to be confident, and even how to have sex in the confinements of marriage. He taught me that a man should be the head of their household and be the priest of the house. Meaning that it is the man's responsibility to lead the family into prayer and to provide and protect the family at all costs. The man will be the spiritual guidance as God would speak to the man and direct him to guide the family. Being a man is not about how old you are or how many women you have been with. It's the ability to live up to the standards that God has called you to and to exude leadership and wisdom.

We should magnify our manhood by leading ourselves and leading our families. Before we can effectively lead anyone, we must first lead ourselves. There must be a list of goals and aspirations that we are striving towards and we must set deadlines to meet them. As we progress, we will find that we become more disciplined and find new opportunities to succeed. Once we can effectively lead ourselves, we must lead our family, friends, and community.

God has created us in His image and likeness. He is known as a powerful being who affects positive change. That is the exact way He wants us to operate; with power and wisdom leading our communities and families to overall success. Also, to provide a shield of protection to protect against evil forces that may arise. As men, we must take action to make a difference and ensure the end goal becomes reality.

As I look back, I realize that I could never have made it so far without forming the right relationships. It is not easy to overcome the hurdles and obstacles we face in life. Sometimes we are met with depression and discouragement. In spite of the negative feelings, we must attempt to develop bonds with other men who can help lift us when we are down. If we are struggling with something, we should find a trusted friend who can be our accountability partner to keep us in check and help us through. I have had a few accountability partners who were able to really effectively help and encourage me through the process. We make the biggest mistakes when we believe we can go it alone. Even the President of the United States needs a team of people who can help and advise him. No one is an island; every one of us needs help.

As we progress in life, we will stumble and experience many setbacks but that does not make us a failure. We have to understand that every opportunity whether successful or not helps us in the long run. We learn from our mistakes and create successful ventures. I am an avid believer that whatever you have a passion for, if you give your all, you can be extremely successful. If you have a desire to clean toilets, you can be a millionaire in doing so because the passion you have will drive you to innovate and create new ways to solve the issue at hand. With passion comes innovation and with persistence comes opportunity.

Since I always had a thing for computers and an interest in information technology (IT), I attended Georgia State University as a computer engineering major. Almost every class I took, I ended up failing or barely making it. It was so dreadful that I thought I had a learning deficiency. So I took a break for three years as I weighed my options. At the time, I worked for Wells Fargo Bank as a part-time teller. I did not have a plan and was petrified of the future. I thought will I be a teller forever? Will I graduate from college? Am I able to provide for my family? I was driven by these questions to try harder despite my reservations. So I worked hard and was able to acquire a promotion every year. I moved from teller to banker to management to corporate without a college degree. With the experience from the financial industry, I went back to Georgia State with a focus in finance and graduated on the President's list.

Although I failed many times I did not allow it to back me into a corner and quit. I pushed through and found what my true passion was. Sometimes it takes hardship to see what is really on the inside. Setbacks can sometimes show us where our passion really resides. Sometimes it takes failure to allow us to appreciate success. When you find what you find your passion, you can be a catalyst for change in that particular industry.

When God created us, His intent was for us to thrive. He made sure that we had everything we needed. Although Adam interrupted the flow, Jesus came to restore us to our rightful place. I have learned that I can be as successful as anyone else in the world. If someone else can do it, so can I. Instead of settling for less and work for someone else, why don't we aspire to be business owners and entrepreneurs? In order to find this success, first we must find a passion. Then we must find a mentor in that field. I cannot stress enough the importance of those two necessities.

There are many challenges and setbacks that are designed to keep us down. As we attempt to move forward, we find persistent opposition and discouraging circumstances. We never seem to find an easy path to victory, but will we ever? We are men! And God has designed us to be strong, wise, ambitious, perseverant and resilient. We have these qualities that will take us through every storm and fire. We should never let any circumstance dishearten us and should fight with everything that God has given us. We magnify our manhood by never giving up and finding value in everything that we do, say and think. Your image is important!

~Dedication~

Justin Davis, Conyers, GA

Christopher Chin, Passaic, NJ

Matthew Reynolds, Brooklyn, NY

Francis Laryea, Athens, GA

Ricky Peart, Stone Mountain, GA

Maxwell Peart, Atlanta, GA

Aaron Stewart, Atlanta, GA

David Lee, Lithonia, GA

Steven Welch, Reading, PA

Nathan McFarlane, Atlanta, GA

Biography of Maurice Edward

While most teenage boys were competing in school sports or chasing girls, Maurice Donte Edwards, formerly known as "DJ Punchline" was consumed by the turntables. Reminiscent of the 80's B-boy DJs spinning records out of crates, Punchline sacrificed all of his free time to honing his craft as first a rapper, then a DJ before his teenage years even began. Punchline quickly adapted to the methods of DJ'ing from spinning and scratching to eventually blending and mixing. Born in the small town of Kinston, North Carolina, August 29, 1988, where everyone knows your name and face, gathering notoriety was not a difficult task. Quickly he was pinned the "Youngest in Charge" from his performances at sold out high school parties, talent shows and proms.

"I been doing parties since I was 15, but then I got a gig on Saturdays at a club for the teenage crowd and they loved me. All day in school, all I could focus on was records. I would play at the end of the week. Some kids wanted to get high and skip class. My high was music and making it to Saturday!"

It wasn't long before Punchline's work ethic was acknowledged by North Carolina's elite DJs, DJ Barry Bee and DJ Skee Money. It was through these chance meetings that DJ Punchline began to realize DJ'ing was not only a skill but also a business. He started his own label, PRC and signed his first artist, Moe Soundz. It was by joining their organization, Nitram Knarf DJs that allowed Punchline to travel statewide spinning for adult hip-hop clubs and meeting celebrity recording artists, such as Trey Songz, Bruce Bruce, Crank Squad, and Rich Boy.

"At first I had to carry the crates and warm the crowd up, but every now and then Barry Bee would need a break and let me step in to do my thang. Even though I was with older people partying, I never felt like I wanted to join in, drink and have fun. I just wanted to get better and better, so I wouldn't leave the booth."

He was also invited to DJ for Big Daddy Kane's protégé', Mica Swain for her birthday party. All this was accomplished by age 18! Constantly in the studio with his own artist and hosting mixtapes for independent artists, Punchline realized his love for rapping would not fade and began recording rap intros for the hottest mix station in the Carolinas, 101.9 Kiss FM. and 92.1 Jams, working under DJ Shon B. His intros and commercials would spin all day but no one recognized it was him because his voice was so mature. Eventually his raps would get longer and his intros started to sound more like songs. It was around this time, Punchline met Miss Ricki, an independent artist consultant and manager who advised him to not only work harder, but work smarter. She advised him to network with DJs from around the country, expand his ear for great music and concentrate on the good and bad of the industry. He began attending music conferences and artist showcases and ran into TJ Chapman, owner of TJs DJs, the largest record pool in the nation and Tony Neal, President of the Core DJs. His witness of their rise from crate carriers to respected businessmen even through failure and setbacks, really placed things in perspective for him.

Senior year was drawing near to an end and with the guidance of his mother, Punchline knew in order to be great, one must follow in the shoes of greatness and have a purpose. Punchline's belief was that no one is greater than God, and by following closely, he would learn his true purpose. And that he did. Shortly after graduation, no longer a boy, becoming a new man, Punchline gave his life to God.

"Without God, life has no purpose. With no purpose, life has no meaning. With no meaning, life has no hope, ya digg?! The old me is dead. The new me is alive. "

Retiring the name DJ Punchline, Maurice now goes by, "MOE Soundz." His passion for music and sounds are vibrant through his gospel raps. But instead of club atmospheres filled with liquor and smoke, Moe Soundz spends his time rapping and motivating children and young adults to be the best version of themselves.

Personal Profile

Key Words

Create, Future, Awesome, Innovation

Favorite Quote

"If you fail to plan, you are planning to fail!" ~Benjamin Franklin

Values

Building Relationships, Networking, Sharing, Teamwork, Awesome Character

Marketable Skills

Business, Sales training, Music Business, Leadership, Teamwork

Contact Information

Email: djm.soundz@gmail.com
Facebook: https://www.facebook.com/maurice.g.edwards
LinkedIn.com: Maurice Edwards

HEY DUDE! IT'S IMPORTANT!

Maurice Edwards

I think manhood is important in our everyday lives; important in our relationships with our mothers, brothers, sisters, girlfriends, wives and friends. Being a strong foundation for the important things in our lives is an unspoken truth that everyone wants in a male. The reason I say unspoken truth is once those truths are broken, then you are labeled as a "bad man." In relationships with a girlfriend or a wife, they are trusting you to help lead them without dictating to them, harming them verbally or physically, and most of all, cheating on them. So many families are broken up just because of those things. A relationship should be meant to bring unity and peace, not an emotional battle with turmoil and destruction. I'm not saying there won't be disagreements, but we have to work it out in better ways.

I told myself if I was to have kids, I would be there to see them grow up. I would be there to watch them play their first drum set. I would be there to buy my daughter her first baby doll. Not only being there in the beginning, but remaining consistent in their lives. When I was growing up, I didn't have my father in my life. Some days I wished he was there and other days I told my mother I would be fine. She never pushed the issue of meeting him, but one day I asked her about him. I wanted to see who my father was and who the man that I was to become is. She told me to wait for a little while and she would find his number. Well, she called him that morning and he was excited to meet with me later that day. We had a great time and we were finally starting to get to know each other. A couple months later something bad happened between us and I didn't want to talk to him for a while. I won't disclose what happened that day, but I called my mom and told her to come get me right then.

Even though my father wasn't in my life in its earlier stages, I still had good role models who spent time with me. Also, I'm truly grateful for friends who helped along the way. One of those good friends was Maurice Manuel. We would hang out and have tons of fun while playing PlayStation and working out. When I started making music, he always listened to my rhymes and beats I made. He wasn't hard on me, but he would tell me I could have done better on this one or that one. It only made me want to go home and work on it every day. I worked harder to make it better than the day before. Maurice was always selling items at the Flea Market, so I started riding with him every weekend, learning how to sell product and conduct business. Other kids where playing outside on the weekend, but not me. I was ready to hop in his car and go make sales. I learned so many things from him; from cutting hair to how to treat people. My mom did the best she could with what she had and I love her for that. She was always there for me and my brother Curtis. Family is important, because when all your friends leave you, family will always be there when you need them. My uncles played an important part in my life as well.

Because they wanted me to do good for myself, they always told me things to look out for while growing up. However, I wish I would've listen a little better. They were so right on many things such as paying attention in school, being on your best behavior in public, and not following after the other kids, but being yourself. When I went to my aunt's house to stay until my mom was done working, Aunt Ernestine and Uncle Phil would tell me to study hard. Uncle Luby would always take me fishing in the summer and Uncle Roscoe would always bring home presents. Those were the good old days and I truly miss them. Also, I had my favorite cousins, Rodney, Chris and Erick, who I couldn't wait to hang out with. I would do anything for them if they asked me.

Every day I push to be a better person since I have Curtis and Cayden to look out for. Spending time and helping them grow is one of my missions. We have good times and bad times but that's a part of life. When they grow up and become successful, that would be awesome for me to see. I encourage all males to spend time with other males. It's critical for our success. Sometimes we don't know what to do or we're caught up with life and need a reality check. We are living in a society where people have hidden agendas and motives. Therefore, I will take tough love any day. This world is full of temptations and trouble that are so easy to be a part of. We all need role models who show us how to seek God and treat our girlfriends and wives. Especially the role models who keep us accountability for our actions.

After barely graduating from high school, most of my time was geared towards music. I helped form a music group with my best friends at the time and traveled to different locations to do shows. We put in the work to enter the entertainment industry by eating and sleeping music for years. I remember a few years back, seeing Puff Daddy dancing in the deceased rapper The Notorious B.I.G.

video on television. Then Bad Boy Entertainment flashed across the screen. Immediately, I said, "I want to be just like him!" He was making music and he was a businessman. I wanted to do it all and more. I believe in having dreams that are worthwhile and having a focus that takes you out of your current situation. It gives you hope in something better. Comedian and entertainer mogul Steve Harvey said, "The dream is free, but the hustle is sold separately." You have to put in the time and effort to bring dreams into reality.

I would stay in the studio for hours, creating new music almost every day. Yet, we lacked a few things. If I could do it over, in my teenager years, I would have taken all the business courses they offered in high school. When I learned marketing in high school, I was good at creating presentations and selling products to people. My first project was marketing a blackberry cell phone to my classmates. I took my time cutting out the pictures from magazines of the different types of black berry devices. Years later, I used those same skills learned in that class and have done some amazing things with some of the companies I've worked for. I became a manager for Walmart and lead over 30 employees. I've sold over $50,000 worth of merchandise as a salesman. There is nothing more fulfilling than setting a goal and achieving it. It is important to set goals and go after them. However, you must put in the work!

I thank God for saving my life from my past. I attended Dr. Calvin Ellison's church one morning and it changed my entire life! Dr. Ellison has been a great mentor to me. One of the biggest things I've learned from him is to learn new things every day. I used to hate reading books with a passion. Since I've known him, he would always read different types of books. So, I opened my first book and I've been reading ever since. Now, I'm hooked on learning new things because there is so much to learn. I went back to school for two years and would go straight to the library after class. I stayed there for hours at a time reading books. I even rented audio books and listened to them in the car. I was on fire! For the first time in my life, I made A's and B's in my classes. My classmates would ask me for answers, which I never had before, since I was the one normally asking while back in high school. I was shocked because I had never applied myself as I should have. But, I knew for a fact it was God who was changing my life. He was bringing people into my life who inspired me other than those I watched on TV.

For all the men out there, we have to go after our dreams with everything within us. If it wasn't for dreamers and people who took action, we wouldn't have a lot things. Can you think of a world without cell phones, computers, appliances and anything that was invented? We would still be going outside to collect firewood! Throughout history, people have invented many things to solve the problems in our lives that occur. Not only has that happened, but doing so created wealth in serving their communities and passed down wealth to their children. Take the time to make your plan and dreams work, but team up with the right people. Also, don't forget to pay it forward by investing in other people's ideas.

Leadership and Teamwork

Leadership is our God-given role; not to pressure people, but to lead and be the foundation that holds it together. Leadership takes the family or company to places they have never been before, to cover them in prayer and lift them up to God. One must remember that in order to accomplish something great, a company or family has to work together as a team or one unit. But it starts with good leadership. *Where no counsel is, the people fall: but in the multitude of counselors there is safety* (Proverbs 11:14, KJV).

Even though you may be in charge or in the leadership role, make sure you give your team credit for what they have done. All team members are looking at the scoreboard. They want to know where the team stands and what is required to win. Winning six championships throughout his career, Michael Jordan is one of the greatest NBA players who ever played. However, he had a great coach and teammates to win championships. Scottie Pippen, Horace Grant, and Dennis Rodman were some of his teammates and these men stands in a class of hall-of-famers themselves. Remember, your team/family is so worth it. We must invest in our families and teams to be successful. There is no doubt we will receive the greatest return on our investment. What is the return? Having happier families with purpose, education and a greater future.

~Dedication~

Marie Edwards Kinston, NC

Curtis Edwards, Kinston, NC

Maurice Manuel Kinston, NC

Bobby Gratham, Blounts Creek, NC

Luby Edwards Kinston, NC

Roscoe Edwards, Fayetteville, NC

Philp Ashford, Kinston, NC

Rodney Ashford, NC

Chris Ashford, Chicago, IL

Marvin Witherspoon, San Diego, CA

Marty Arnold, Atlanta, GA

Moses Pitt, Kinston, NC

Dr. Calvin Ellison, Stone Mountain, GA

Corey Baker, Greenville, NC

Biography of Thomas Gadsden

Thomas Gadsden was born in Brooklyn NY, attended high school there for two years, and then he moved to Staten Island, NY. He attended Wagner High School in Staten Island and graduated 1985.

After high school he worked as a salesman/service manager for Electrolux. While working at Electrolux, Thomas built a carpet cleaning business. He wanted to do more than just carpet cleaning, so he decided to go to school to become a certified electrician. Thomas is now a certified electrician.

Thomas also worked in a nursing home and after a few years, he decided he wanted more. So he went to work in the hospital and is currently working in the emergency room as a Personal Care Technician for over 20 years.

Thomas is a person of ambition and he decided that he wanted to build a business that he would be able to leave his family as an inheritance. Thomas loves working with his hand and he is very creative so he decided to use all he knew to build the business he loves today. Thomas Gadsden is a licensed General Contractor in New York and in New Jersey and has his own business with a partner. The business is call Rhemah Consultant & Associates, Inc.

Thomas loves to motivate people when he speaks to them. He likes to reach out to people and participate in whatever he can to help in the church and in the community.

Thomas likes bike riding and played sports such as basketball, football, handball, boxing, gymnastics, tracking field, and soccer.

Thomas is a family man. He is married to his lovely wife Sebastiana Rojas-Gadsden. He has two children and two stepchildren from his first marriage. He also has five stepchildren, twelve step grandchildren, and four step great grandchildren with his second marriage. Thomas likes spending time with his family and going on vacations with the family. He is a giver and gives to his family mentally, physically and spiritually.

Thomas is the First Ambassador in New York City for Men Magnifying Manhood. He is looking forward to doing great things with the men. He is also the co-author of two books.

Personal Profile

Key Words
Empowerment, Motivation, Love, Successes, Change

Favorite Quote
Whatever you do in life, it is exactly what you get out of it. So, *keep on keeping on.* Meaning if you do good things in life, good things will come out of it; and if you do bad things in life, bad things will come out of it. It is your choice; therefore, use wisdom.

Values
Family, Friends, Relationship, Compassion, Health

Marketable Skills
Teamwork, Good Listener, Problem Solver, Craftsman, Builder

Contact Information
Thomas Gadsden
Staten Island, New York
Email: tgadsden499@aol.com
Facebook: facebook.com/Thomas Gee

THERE ARE PROBLEMS
AND
THERE ARE SOLUTIONS

Thomas Gadsden

My story begins when I was a young boy growing up in Brooklyn, New York. I grew up with both of my parents until the age of nine. I remember the day my father took me, my younger brother, and my mother down to Charleston, South Carolina to visit his family. We were only supposed to stay for a couple of weeks, but we ended up staying much longer. This was the first time I ever saw my father abuse my mother, not physically but mentally. My father impregnated another woman and man, it really hurt my mother. He kicked us out of his relative's house and we had nowhere to go. We were living on the street until a friend of my father took us to live in a rooming house, which had six large size rooms and one humongous kitchen that everyone shared. My mother, brother and I shared one room because there were other families sharing the other rooms; one room per family. Seeing my father do that to my mother did something to me. You see, at the age of nine I told myself I never wanted to be like my farther.

A year and a half later and now fatherless, we eventually made our way back to Brooklyn. I wanted to help my mother so I got a job bagging groceries. I was 10 and a half making $7.00 a week. During this time, our neighbor asked my mother to go to church with her but she kept refusing. But one day she said to my mother, "Can I take your kids to church?" And my mother said yes, but I didn't know anything about church. I remember when I went that Sunday, we got into trouble. Because we had never seen anyone shouting or praising God, my siblings and I started laughing. The pastor asked if anyone wanted to be baptized, but no one said anything. So I jumped up like the people shouting and said, "Me, me, me!" I didn't know what baptism meant. I thought I was volunteering to help someone else, not knowing I was helping myself which would later help me in my spiritual walk.

So years go by and now I am a teenager in high school in Brooklyn. The thing I remember about my high school was not the sports I played, but trying to avoid getting into fights in the hallways, after the class bell rung. If you were caught fighting, the security guards would take both boys into the bathroom so they could fight it out. But my high school year changed when I moved to Staten Island. I tried to bring what I did in Brooklyn to the school on Staten Island, but things were different. The students didn't wait for the class bell to ring to fight in the hallways, but instead ran into the classroom...to learn. That felt weird to me. I took notice and learned that the teachers and students did care about actually learning. When I signed up to go to the school on Staten Island, they didn't know what grade I was in because my average was a zero. They wanted to put me back in the 9th grade, but my mother said no way. So, I had to take a test and they put me in the 10th grade. I really do believe I belonged in the 11th grade though. So I had to change my attitude, my ways, my thinking, and start going to class. I learned a lot and realized that going to school and class was awesome.

On graduation day, the guidance counselor surprised me with a gift. He stood up and made a speech about how he met this student on the first day and that he attended that school. He went on further to say, "Now this student had an average that I have never seen before, and that was a zero. But here today, on graduation day, he is graduating with the average of 92 and that student is Thomas Gadsden." Everyone started clapping. He called me to come up on the stage, and I did. Then to my surprise, he continued to say, "We are presenting Thomas Gadsden with a full two-year scholarship to Canton College." I was shocked, speechless and started to cry. Now high school was over and real life began.

I started working at a daycare center, but I also enjoyed helping people in my neighborhood especially the elderly living in the senior citizen housing and helping at the Community Center. One summer the daycare had a summer youth work program where they hired high school kids to work at the daycare. The director asked if one of the high school students could come work with me and I said yes. When I started working with the young man, I became friends with him at work. He would talk to me and I realized that he did not have a direction in life. He lived with his mother and two brothers with no father. This young man and I talked every day that summer about doing something that he would love to do with his life. Guess what?! The young man went to school and he became an electrician. That was over 20 years ago and today, that young man and I are still friends. We talk, call each other once in a while, go out to dinner and he also attends church with me. So, I guess I empowered this young man to do something with his life. You see by me speaking a positive word into this young man's life, he turned out to be a responsible working young man.

I also have a stepson and was very involved in his life and I did a lot of things with him. When he became a teenager, he started having certain problems. Even though he was going the wrong way, I didn't

86

give up on him. He told his mother he could never forget the things I did with him as a child and even as a teenager. Today he is 28 years old, has gotten his life together, and still comes to me for advice. He is a supervisor at a facility for young men and women who need help with daily living. It is an awesome thing when we can empower our own family.

As men, we all should take time out of our busy schedules to empower young men of any age, a young or older adult. I believe that there will be less or no gangs and fewer men in prison if we would take the time out to let them know there is more to life than prison and gang life. God has a purpose for all men in the world today. We might not know what that purpose is, but to understand that purpose, we must first have a spiritual relationship with God. He will teach us about our purpose through the physical, mental, and spiritual problems we face.

We must realize and know that to every problem, there is a solution. The problem and the solution in the world today start with the person in the mirror. That person can be the one who started the problem or the one who solves the problem. Which one are you? I said that to say this. There are a lot of different problems today. I know we all have our different problems: **physical problems, mental problems**, and also **spiritual problems**. Believe me, there is a solution to all of these problems. The definition of problem is a situation that is unsatisfactory difficulties for people.

Physical Problems

Let us talk a little about the physical problem. Now men, there is a high percentage of us who would put off our physical health because we have a lack of patience. Let me tell you a story. I work in a hospital in the emergency room. One day I remembered that I had to work on Father's Day. I was working in the trauma area and three different cases came in three different times, but the three cases had to do with three men with similar conditions. They were diagnosed with having a heart attack, but they came into the emergency room on the same day but at different times. Now when you are diagnosed with having a heart attack, you have to go through some tests to be certain it is a heart attack. One of the men that came in did not want to wait for the test results. He did not have the patience to wait for the doctor to come into the room to see him and he decided to sign himself out of the hospital against the doctor's advice. 30 to 45 minutes went by when he was brought back to the hospital, but this time he was brought back by paramedics as they performed chest compressions. The doctor and staff took over and they started working on him, but he was unresponsive. After a while, they pronounced him dead. This young man was in his early forties. If he'd only just stayed and waited for those tests and the doctor to see him, he would probably be alive today.

The keyword in this story is patience. How many of us men have this type of patience? In the Bible, we see that suffering and patience often go hand in hand. The great thing about this is that God promises our suffering will produce endurance, character, and hope (Romans 5:3-5).

Here are a few examples of patience in the Bible regarding Abraham and Sarah (Genesis 15:1- 6 Genesis 17:15; 21:1-8). I would love to tell you guys about the Scriptures, but I need you to go through the Bible and search the Scriptures for yourself to experience what I have experienced and learned about patience.

Mental Problems

The definition of *mental* is of or relating to the mind specifically: of or relating to the total emotional and intellectual response of an individual to external reality. There are different types of mental situations such as mental illness, mental breakdown, mental disorder, and mental patient. When we hear these types of mental

88

situations, we think of the word "crazy." What about mental ideas, mental science, or a mental note? So, when you hear these types of mental words, do you think of the word "crazy" now? There is another word that comes from *mental* and that is *mentally*. The definition for *mentally* basically is in the mind or using the mind. To better yourself or to help better someone else, you must change your mindset first. I changed my mindset by reading the Bible and inspirational books.

I read in a book that said, "You cannot have a positive life and a negative mind." The Bible says in Romans 8:5-8, "For those who live according to the flesh set their minds on things of the flesh, but those who live according to the spirit set that minds on the things of the Spirit. For to set the mind on the flesh is death, but to set the mind on the spirit is life and peace. For the mind that is set on the flesh is hostile to God, for it does not submit to God's law; indeed, it cannot. Those who are in the flesh cannot please God."

There are a lot of Scriptures in the Bible that can help you change your mindset, such as Colossians 3:2; Matthew 25:34; 1Timothy 6:6-9; and Galatians 6:1-6. Please take a moment and read these Scriptures.

Spiritual Problems

Spiritual problems are not only for spiritual people. I read in a spiritual study guide that 80% of our problems are spiritual. So does that means 20% of our problems are physical? Let us say if this was reversed and 20% was spiritual and 80% was physical, what would that mean? It means there is a *solution* for the 80% and the 20%. Now the percentage on how many people are not spiritual, that I do not know. What I do know is that 80% of our problem is spiritual. We need to know how to deal with the spiritual problems. I do believe we all should first confess out of our mouth that Jesus is our Lord and Savior. That would be a start because it takes just more than recognizing that Jesus is our Lord and Savior. When it comes to spiritual problems, we need help, not from a physical person, but from GOD! If 80% of the problems in the world today are spiritual, we the people who play a big part in that.

Listen to this. The problems in the world today are not political or economic. The problems in the world today are spiritual. They have to do with what you believe. They have to do with our most inner thoughts and ideas about life, about God, about ourselves, and how we are living today. Therefore, it is extremely important to know what the Bible says about problems. Here are some Scriptures:

Nehemiah 8:10 - *Do not grieve, for the joy of the lord is your strength. Isaiah 41:10 so do not fear, for I am with you; do not be dismayed, for I am your God. I will strengthen you and help.*

Exodus 15:2 - *The Lord is my strength and my song; he has given me victory.*

Why is it, when we hear the word *problem*, our first instinct is to think negative? Think about this. Do you think God allows things to happen to us? Not to kill, destroy or break us down but to strengthen us. For instance, let's say you were in a car accident. You are driving down the street when the light turns green and you keep going. Your car gets hit by an 18-wheeler and all 18 wheels roll over your car and flatten your car. However, you only come out of it with a broken arm. Is that a blessing? Oh, I know what you are thinking! You are thinking that the accident still happened. Yes, the accident did happen and you only came out with a broken arm. God allowed that accident to happen, but He did not allow you to die in that accident! Now take a second and think about that!

Time After Time

I can count on one hand how time after time God spared my life. He gave me numerous chances and I thank Him every day that He allows me to wake up each morning. I thank Him every day that He allows me to get through the day. When I am going through my problems, I pray about it and I put my problems in God's hands. You know the best thing you can do is to go to God and ask Him for His help, because remember 80% of our problems are spiritual. And even if the 20% is not spiritual, God still can help you. Because there is nothing that He cannot do.

The Bible says *"You are the salt of the earth. But if the salt loses its saltiness, how can it be made salty again. It is no longer good for anything, except to be thrown out and trampled underfoot. 14. You are the light that gives light to the world. A town built on hill cannot be hidden. 15. Neither do people light a lamp and put it under a bowl. Instead they put it on its stand, and it gives light to everyone in the house. 16. In the same way, let your light shine before others, that they may see your good deeds and glorify your Father in heaven.* (Matthew 5:13-16, NIV)

We all must change our mindset. For us to empower the next person, we must work on the person in the mirror. Because:

- If you believe you are beaten, you are.

- If you believe you dare not, you do not.

- If you believe you're losing, you've lost.

You see believing and mindset are a team. Now you need to believe that you can change your mindset; so let your team go to work. I changed my mindset by trusting and believing in God. I pray and ask Him to give me the wisdom when I am ministering to the few brothers I know who are in lock up and the ones who are not. With God on my team, it is a win-win situation. I just want to thank you for taking the time out of your busy schedule to read this book. This book will give you the tools and the wisdom to empower you and your brothers and sisters. Thank you and God bless!

~Dedication~

Sebastiana-Rojas Gadsden, Staten Island, NY

Alyssamae Gadsden, Staten Island, NY

Thomas Gadsden Jr, Staten Island, NY

Apostle Leonard Edward, Linden, NJ

Yvette Edward, Linden, NJ

Christopher Esteves, Staten Island, NY

Tim Gadsden, Bronx, NY

Jimmy Paniagua, Englewood, FL

Nicole Paniagua, Englewood, FL

Biography of Johnell Gibbs

Johnell Gibbs, is an inspiring Life Coach, Health Coach, and Motivational Speaker. He has come to develop a heart for helping youth, and seeing their level of development rise. His passion lies within watching individuals discover their gifts and find themselves in Christ. The process of self-discovery is what fuels him to perfect his craft in the goal to achieve all of his aspirations. While going through the process of growing up with an absent father, he was able to put all of the hardship to good use and use it to find his passion. In the process to find himself, he continues to pour himself into his relationship with God and put himself in positions to achieve the success he wishes to pass down to others.

In his early life, Johnell attended Hillside High School, and finished at Mount Zion Christian Academy which helped with the process of an early foundation in the Word of God. There, they provided him with the necessary tools to succeed. He now looks to continue on his path by obtaining a degree in theology and nutrition, in hopes to be in servitude to the world around him. He also hopes that this will help him on the path to help aid in the transformative lifestyle experiences of others. He ultimately wants his actions to bring all glory to God in everything he does.

Personal Profile

Key Words

Passion, Motivation, Confidence, Love, Leadership

Favorite Quote

"You can fail at what you don't want, so you might as well take a chance on doing what you love."

Values

Love, Character, Integrity, Vision, Purpose, Destiny

Marketable Skills

Leadership, Problem Solving, Trustworthy, Empowerment, Goal Oriented

Contact Information

Email: johnellgibbsjr@hotmail.com

Instagram: johnellgibbsjr

YouTube: Johnell Gibbs Jr

A YOUNG MAN WITH VISION, PURPOSE, AND DESTINY

Johnell Gibbs

First and foremost, I want to give glory and honor to God Almighty. Second, I want to thank my parents for conceiving me into the world. Third, I want to thank my Pastor and First Lady of Mount Zion Christian Church for their undying faithfulness to the ministry and for everything that they have deposited into me over these twenty-two years. And, last but not least, I want to give a big thanks to Dr. Calvin Ellison for this huge opportunity to be a part of something as magnificent as this, and I hope that everything that is written in this book becomes life changing. Now with all that being said, let's dive in!

Having a "father" lays that foundation for your entire life and most men who grow up without a father never gain a sense of identity hints the identity crisis we face in the world today. The title of this is called A "Young Man with Vison, Purpose, and Destiny" because for the most part of my youth, I wondered through life aimlessly. I was never really conscious of everything that went on around me or everything I took part in. The absence of my father naturally left a void that needed to be filled. In his absence, there were talks we never had, quality time that was never given or received, lessons that were never learned, and love that was never shown. In the book of 1 Kings, David is about to die and he is leaving everything to the soon to be King Solomon. When David's time to die drew near, he commanded Solomon, saying, *I am about to go the way of all the earth. Be strong, and show yourself a man, and keep the charge of the Lord your God, walking in his ways and keeping his statutes, his commandments, his rules, and his testimonies, as it is written in the Law of Moses, that you may prosper in all that you do and wherever you turn, that the Lord may establish his word that he spoke concerning me, saying, 'If your sons pay close attention to their way, to walk before me in faithfulness with all their heart and with all their soul, you shall not lack[a] a man on the throne of Israel. (1Kings 2:2-4)*

In the New International Version (NIV), the verse reads, *I am about to go the way of all the earth.* He said, *So be strong, 'act' like a man.*

In the Amplified Bible (AMP), the verse reads, *I am going the way of all the earth [as dust to dust]. Be strong and 'prove' yourself a man.*

In the Message Bible (MSG), the verse reads, *I'm about to go the way of all the earth, but you—be strong; 'show' what you're made of! Do what God tells you.*

Each version uses a different word to express what David was saying to his son. To act, prove, and to show himself as a man. For a father to teach the lesson of to act, prove, and to show is to give a young man the basic foundation of manhood. For a young man to act, he is performing a thing; an action. Which is a deed that is being done or carried out; the process of doing something. For one to prove is to learn or find out by experience. Most use this in a way to test a certain theory that you have been taught to establish the existence, truth, or validity of (as by evidence or logic); to search for truth behind a belief. To show is to cause or permit to be seen; to exhibit a certain type of behavior and to present as a public spectacle.

David was telling Solomon, *"It's your time now."* I have taught you since a child and I have set a standard for you to live by, and I've been an example for you. Now it's time for you to know God for yourself. It is time for you to put God to the test, as you have seen what God has done for me. So now it's all on you my son; it's time for you to **act, prove, and show** yourself a man.

We must understand that back in biblical times, it was tradition to pass down something that was of extreme importance and value as seen throughout the entire Bible. God passed down dominion, David passed down a throne, and Jesus Christ passed down salvation. Whereas for us, when a father passes down something to a young man it gives him a sense of identity; it gives him a clear direction for his life, and it ultimately gives the sense of vision, purpose, and destiny.

Like many young men in this day and time, I went without a male role model to look up to. I had no one to lead me, guide me, and be that strong, foundational figure in my life. Without a role model to pass down manhood to me, came many of my life-changing struggles. I battled addictions, pain, confusion of life, and much, much more. During the beginning, I was aimlessly wondering in my youth, because I was lost and had no direction for myself. My actions were led by the societal influences that I believed "made you into a man." I began to realize that my actions were no longer 100%

my own, seeing as they were now being led by perception. I smoked weed, I popped pills, I cursed, I masturbated, watched porn, all because I thought these to be the true actions of *men*. I treated young girls like trash instead of treating them delicately, and respectfully because I was never taught how a man was to properly treat his girl. I even questioned my sexuality because all around me I saw men changing their sexuality and acting indifferent to their gender. All of my actions went based off the influences of society, not lessons from a respected role model. Our society delivers an entirely different view of the concept of passing something down to the next generation. One of the biggest reasons for this, is a lack of fathers in the home, in our communities, and a lack of father's nationwide. Though, it's no secret that you can be a father, but not a *real* father. You can be a man, but not a *real* man. You can be a leader, but not a *real* leader. There are things that need to be resolved in us as men if we are to rise and become more.

There is a verse in the last chapter of Malachi, that reads, *And he shall turn the heart of the fathers to the children, and the heart of the children to their fathers, lest I come and smite the earth with a curse* (Malachi. 4:6). As men we have lost our connection with our true Father. In return, this is the cause for all the problems that we see in the world today. What does that mean exactly... *"To lose our connection with our true father?"* To truly understand, we must go back to where it all started; "the Garden of Eden" where we as males began. *"Now the Lord God had planted a garden in the east, in Eden; and there he put the man that he had formed"* (Genesis 2:8). God didn't "put the man that he had formed" just anywhere; he put him in a specific place, The Garden of Eden. In the book *"Understanding The Purpose and Power of Men"* written by Dr. Myles Munroe, he stated Eden comes from the Hebrew word, meaning "delicate, delight, or pleasure." The word garden means "an enclosure or something "fenced in." The Garden was essentially

God's incubator for man. It was a place where God wanted to keep us close to Him, because Eden was a place where God's presence was in direct contact with man. Dr. Munroe went on to say, *"A central reason that God placed the male in the garden was so that he could be in his presence all the time. He could walk and talk with the Lord in the cool of the day. He could hear God's voice. This was a place where communion, fellowship, and oneness with God was always intact."*

Now, there is an analogy that I have come across, of a manufacturer and his product; with us being the product and God being the Manufacturer. You can't take an Apple product to a Microsoft store, a Mercedes product to a Lexus dealership, and you can't take a Rolex to a G-shock company. This is all because you're looking to someone to make a fix when they're not the manufacturer. God never intended for Adam to move from the garden (His presence). He wanted Adam to take the garden (His presence), and spread it throughout the world. This is what God meant when He said, *"have dominion over the earth"* (Genesis 1:28). His purpose in doing this was for Adam to take this prototype of life and transform it into an actual system of life that He intended for the world to live by. In reference to Isaiah 11: 9 (KJV), *"They shall not hurt nor destroy in all my holy mountain: for the earth shall be full of the knowledge of the LORD, as the waters cover the sea."* This was essentially saying that this could not successfully be executed, without Adam being in good communications with God, the Manufacturer. In essence, when our connection with our manufacturer was lost, we also lost our foundation that was instilled in us upon creation. There was a sense of identity that was lost, forcing us to become beings without **vision, purpose, and destiny**.

The reason for all the confusion, and the reason why men are lost in society is because of this very reason. Jails are filled with our men, women are left without support, wives and children are beaten by the men of the house, and manhood is in turmoil and has lost its value and respect. The definition of being a father has taken a turn over time, for the worst. Where kids used to look up to their fathers as role models, they now look up to their mothers or to role models who they see on television. Men used to be the foundation of the home, and now their absence has left that job vacant, forcing others in the house to pick up the pieces. Being a man has lost all significance. All due to the loss of communication with the Manufacturer. There has to be a way to go about regaining our morality as men. The simplicity of the solution is usually shocking. God created everything with order attached to it. Every creation has order and purpose; the same way stars need firmaments, because without them, they would burn up. Aquatic animals need water to survive, and plants need soil to take root, and man needs God to walk the simplified path.

I believe that for us as men to regain our footing, we must regain our relationship with our Creator. He is the one, who knows us from the inside and out. Our friends don't know us, and the drugs we use can't help us find out who we are. The women we sleep with don't know us, and can't help fill the void that we feel inside. No matter what we do, there will always be an empty hole in our lives that none of these temporal things can fill. Why is it that no matter what we do nothing can complete us the way the Creator can? The answer to that question is found in the book of Psalms..."*For you formed my inward parts; you knitted me together in my mother's womb*" (Psalm 139:13). David was saying to the Existent God, "You know me from the inside and out. You know my deepest darkest secrets; you know what I love and what I hate. You know when I'm happy, and when I'm sad. You are my Creator; You complete me, God!" The writer of Ecclesiastes (King Solomon) said it best..."*he has put eternity into man's heart*" (Ecclesiastes 3:11). God has put a deep longing for something more on the inside of men. It does not matter what we do or where we go; we will always have this deep longing for more. Every man on this planet from young to old, rich to poor, from the believer to the non-believer, we all have this eternal itch that we just can't seem to satisfy. That's why we drink so much, that why we fornicate so much, that's why we get high out of our minds because ultimately, we are trying to find refuge in some other resource that can never give us what we need; except our True Source: God. He is that answer to all your questions. He is the only one who will ever complete you, and He is the true source who we spend our whole lives looking for. It is in Him you live, in Him you move, and in Him you have your very being.

I don't want to sit here and preach to you or bore you with Scripture, but this is the only way I can relay the message that I am trying to get across to you. We spend our whole lives going through things as men whether mental, physically, or emotionally and we never really deal with the true problem. We are hurt, we feel abandoned, and we're scared. Our pride and confidence is even scared; leading us to go every day with this fake shield up and trying to pretend that everything is alright. When in fact, we are far from it. I recently went out to eat with a mentor from church and we hadn't hung out in a while, so we just began to catch up. He asked me what I had been up to, and what was going on in my life. I told him and before I could finish, he stopped me and said something that I really needed to hear: "You're not a failure, and once you begin to believe that, you'll do great things." He said something that had been on my mind. For as long as I could remember, I felt like a failure and even when people would compliment me and tell me how wonderful I was, I would still feel like a flat out failure. I am telling you this because I know that there is someone who is out there with that same feeling. On the outside, you portray yourself to be this overly confident, cocky, arrogant guy, but deep down inside, you feel like a failure. You feel as though you'll never amount to anything and not matter what you do, it's not good enough. There are plenty of men who feel this way and or think this way. Whether your father abandoned, abused, rejected, or just dismissed you all together, we have to confront these feelings. We can no longer run from these feelings because look at the state that we're in guys! This is me pouring my deepest feelings out to you all; raw authenticity. We have sex trafficking on the rise, people killing one another, suicide is rising at an alarming rate, and kids are being molested by the very people who should be there to protect them. Our country is in shambles! We cannot continue to allow this to go on. It's time to confront these problems within ourselves, and get to the root of the problem and the root is us…men. We are the reason we see our world flipped and turned upside down. This is the result of us having lost our foundation, morals, and our direct contact with our Manufacturer. We don't know what to do with our lives; searching for answers in the wrong places.

It's time for us to return back to the Manufacturer, and regain what was lost. It's time for us to reestablish the connection with the spirit of manhood. To find the solution, go to the one who came to help us regain out spirit of leadership, manhood, and ultimately, our spirit of dominion: Jesus Christ. He is the only who can restore you; He is that only one who can lead you directly to the Creator. *"I am the way, and the truth, and the life. No one comes to the Father* (Manufacturer) *except through me"* (John 14:6). Jesus knows the truth about who we truly are, that is why we turn to Him for restoration. It's not about religion, but it's about rediscovering what we lost. I must tell you this crucial part. The coming of Christ was not the coming of a religion as people may believe. It was a reestablishment of a Kingdom. The first thing Christ said when He stepped on the scene was *"Repent, for the Kingdom of heaven is at hand."* He told His disciples, *"I confer on you a kingdom, just as my Father conferred one on me."* When you confer something on someone, you are granting or bestowing a certain title, degree, benefit, or right to them. Jesus was telling the men who He was teaching, *"I'm giving you back your kingdom rights; I'm giving you back your kingdom title."*

"And it shall come to pass afterward, that I will pour out my spirit upon all flesh; and your sons and your daughters shall prophesy, your old men shall dream dreams, your young men shall see visions" (Joel 2: 28, KJV). There is a lot to be said within this verse, but the significance to be distinguished from this verse comes from *"old men will dream dreams, young men shall see visions."* It was said that the Spirit would come upon all, but there is a specific thing that will happen to men. This isn't to take away from anyone else, but it's being said that when the Lord's Spirit is poured out, His Spirit is coming to give you your dream and your vision back. If you can bring yourself to gain the spirit of dominion, leadership, character, and manhood, you will truly realize what you have in God. It is then, when you can become a man with **vision, purpose, and destiny.** You can become a "Man Magnifying Manhood!"

~Dedication~

Mykel Marks, Durham, NC

John Hargrave, High Point, NC

Tyler Evans, Durham, NC

Kenard Johnson, Rocky Mount, NC

Josh Scarborough, Durham, NC

Donnell Gibbs, Chapel Hill, NC

Raheem Patrick, New York, NY

Gary Robinson Jr., Fayetteville, NC

Christopher Braswell, Rocky Mount, NC

Joab Ham, Durham, NC

Sterling Mason, Durham, NC

Jordan Burnett, Durham, NC

Eric Price Jr., Upper Marlboro, MD

Quentin Henderson, Durham, NC

Biography of Bishop Arlan Gibson

Bishop Arlan Gibson is an author and Pastor Emeritus of Shades of God Christian Center. He is a graduate of Beulah Heights University, with a Bachelor of Arts in Religious Studies. He is a member of Grace Church International under the leadership of Bishop Jonathan Alvarado, where he serves as the Director of the Men's Ministry. He previously attended New Birth Missionary Baptist Church where he led The New Birth Business Association for many years.

Arlan is the Founder and CEO of Infinity Global Energy, LLC. As a proud Vietnam Veteran, Arlan is an active member of the American Legion Post 77 and the Veterans of Foreign Wars, Post 5290. Arlan is a community activist and a former member of the Rockdale Chamber of Commerce. He and his wife volunteer as Facilitator's for Radical Love Marriage Ministry of Hopewell Missionary Baptist Church.

Personal Profile

Key Words

Compassion, Community, Generational, Men, Marriage

Favorite Quote

I can do all things through Christ who strengthens me.
(Philippians 4:13)

Values

Do unto others as you would have them do to you.
Forgiveness, Compassion

Marketable Skills

Public Speaking, Marriage Facilitator, Leadership

Contact Information

Email: Arlan.gibson61@gmail.com

Website: www.arlangibson.net

Facebook: facebook.com/Arlan Gibson Speaker/Author

FROM FORTUNATE SON TO PRODIGAL SON

Bishop Arlan Gibson

Ooh, they send you down to war, Lord
And when you ask them, "How much should we give?"
Ooh, they only answer "More! More! More!" Yoh
It ain't me, it ain't me, I ain't no military son, son
It ain't me, it ain't me, I ain't no fortunate one, one
~Fortunate Son, Creedence Clearwater Revival

I was asked to contribute a chapter to this amazing book in the hopes that my personal story could inspire someone else to make more out of the talents and experiences they have been given. He asked if I could "share my testimony," which to those of us who have been raised up or come home to a church means something very profound. We are being asked to share with other people the inner workings of probably the two most personal relationships we have in our lives, our relationship with our Maker and our relationship with ourselves. How does one even start? I could tell you that I was born in St. Louis, Missouri during the baby boom, that my mother died giving birth to me, and that I eventually moved to New Jersey with her family but it's probably more important to tell you that I first received Christ at the age of nine. That's where this story begins because that is when all of my inheritance was bestowed upon me. Now let me tell you how I briefly lost it.

I grew up during an era of the United States when people were coming to terms with issues of wealth, sex, and race. It was a time of internecine struggles for the soul of the country. Questions were being asked that no one had asked in the nation's two hundred years. It was also a time when we were drafting young men and sending them across the globe to fight people they'd never even heard about before they got their letter in the mail. I was one of those young men. At 19 years old, I entered the United States Army and was sent to fight a war I didn't understand against people who hadn't done a thing to me.

I don't often speak about Vietnam because describing war to those who have not been is extremely difficult and those who have don't need a recap. I'd rather discuss how easy it is to lose yourself to despair and how difficult it seems to try and find the remnants of your humanity among the ashes because that is a very human predicament to be in. The truth is that I was still a kid in my head when I was sent across the world to kill people. I went from an urban environment to a jungle environment, from an English-speaking country with one set of customs to a place with a wholly different culture, language, and religion. What's worse is that I was there not to appreciate them, but to kill them. That is extremely hard on the spirit. I eventually dealt with my fear, sadness, and bitterness about being in Vietnam among easily accessible drugs. While in Vietnam, I developed an addiction and dependency on heroin that would haunt me the better part of my life.

I use the word "haunt" because it's the most accurate description of drug dependency. Even when you force yourself to get clean and get past the chemical dependency, you're still haunted by the drug mentally. It's there like a specter influencing your whole life. There's dinner with grandma…and heroin. You go to the movies with friends…and heroin. Drugs begin to take on a personality and influence nearly every aspect of your life until you're no longer the person you were but someone entirely different. Heroin replaced my family and defined me with more power and resiliency than my last name did. And when that happens, when you become defined by something outside yourself that you cannot control, it feels like all is lost. Game over. No more quarters. All your extra lives got spent.

Being addicted to heroin is an experience that I would not ever place upon even my worst enemy. In the beginning there is some pleasure and "freedom" from the pain of the world around you, but that doesn't last. That party stops fairly early on and all that's left is the mess to clean up. You get to the point where there is no pleasure only physical pain and illness if you don't do it. That's when the shame sets in and you start your downward spiral of secrecy and isolation. How can you possibly go to church with your grandmother when you're thinking about heroin? How do you eat macaroni and cheese at a family reunion when you're thinking about heroin? You feel like everything that was a part of your world before exists somewhere else and you are barred from that place because you are a heroin addict. Unclean. Dirty.

It was in those moments of despair and hopelessness that I realized all the promises and gifts that were presented to me in that church when I was nine and accepting the Lord as my Savior. I had wealth beyond means. I was rich without measure. There I was far, far from that home I knew and loved, alone and frightened, living with the knowledge that at any moment I could get a bad bag and this addiction would kill me. But I was ready to die. I had accepted that it could happen and sadly, believed I deserved it.

It always seems that it is in those moments of absolute clarity and darkness that even the tiniest light shines bright. In a dark room, a single candle can be seen with the brilliance of sunlight. I was able to see and hear the voices and prayers of those faithful women of my youth, of Miss Mariah Tharrington and Mother Sue Crudup like a beacon in the distance calling me home. The Bible says that faith is the substance of things hoped for and the evidence of things not seen. In that moment I hoped for better. I recalled the Word. I saw in my mind that there was power in forgiveness and I could return to my home, to my faith if I could just learn to forgive myself.

The Kingdom of God is one of spiritual wealth. You cannot buy happiness. You cannot buy love. You cannot buy the feeling you get when you see your child smile at you for the first time. All of the very best things in life cannot be bought with money, only with the fruit of our spirit. I had wealth and I squandered it. I wasted that portion that was entrusted to me. But I had a Father who missed me and waited on me. He wasn't angry that I had walked away from my inheritance; He was saddened. His love is eternal and unshaken by the breaking of time itself and He was waiting for my return. Because He knew I would.

In the tenth chapter of John, Jesus says, *"I give unto them eternal life; and they shall never perish, neither shall any man pluck them from my hand. My Father, which gave them me, is greater than all; and no man is able to pluck them from my Father's hand."*

Take comfort in knowing that Someone's got you. Not only are you safe from some stranger snatching you up, but you can't even take yourself away once God's got you in His hand. I was coming home. There was no doubt about that. Just *when* was the question.

I wouldn't wish either war or heroin on anyone but at this stage in my life, I also wouldn't change a thing about my past. I wouldn't go back and remove either experience because those things made me who I am. I learned about the real meaning of salvation and its boundless value. Mercy, forgiveness, and eternal love---*that* is what I was given. To go back to an earlier analogy, I suddenly had multiple chances to play the game until I could figure out a way to win. Perhaps, more importantly I learned that the game must be played in order to win a prize. I went from being the "Fortunate Son" to the "Prodigal Son" and I will never again lose sight of my real wealth. I had to lose it, to gain it.

I don't know where you are in your life right now, if you're still at home dining on that fatted calf, if you're out wasting your portion, or if you are in the process of making that decision to return home. Heck, you could even be that lucky child who never left the house and hasn't had to deal with the slings and arrows of this world! Whatever state you are in when you read this chapter, all I ask is that you think about that wealth God put aside for you and those talents that He placed upon you at your birth and then ask yourself: *What am I to do with this?*

If you, like me, detoured from what you believe was God's plan for you, I want you to understand that God in His perfection will find a way for you to achieve that plan if you embrace your mission and seed it with a tiny bit of hope and faith. If you don't believe in God or a Higher Power, then I would ask you to look around at the vast potential of the world and the universe that it spins across and realize that there are many solutions to every problem. You may be going through some hard times. Things might look bleak. But trust me when I say that they are not hopeless. You have within you unlimited potential and power to change your life at this very moment.

Though I am a Christian, I like to read about other religions. One of the attributions of the Buddha is: *You as much as anyone in the entire Universe is deserving of your own love.*
Whether he said it or not, I like it. Oftentimes we compare ourselves and our struggle to that of others in order to determine how much time, effort, and attention we give to our own goals and dreams. How many times have you denied your heartache because others have it worse? Or not allowed yourself to be happy about a success because there are other people out there who live without? *Don't complain, now, there's always someone out there that has it worse!* I never knew my mother. I went to war. I was addicted to heroin. Knowing all that I know about my own life I can acknowledge that there are people who had it and have it worse. Mothers in refugee camps so malnourished that they cannot feed the baby at their breast or the man dying of pancreatic cancer—they do exist. But we cannot use them as an excuse or crutch to not take the baton that God is holding out for you. We can manifest the promise God put within us and in doing so potentially act in a way that will change other people's lives in the future.

You have a talent. You have *talents*. You have purpose. You have wealth. You have everything you need right now to take those opportunities around you and run with them to a bold new future for yourself. I'm there to tell you that you don't have to have a testimony like mine to have a testimony. Whatever it is you have been through in life is your private library of knowledge that will come in handy later, either for yourself or those around you. I had a Marine tell me once, "You've survived one hundred percent of the things that might have killed you already. You can survive some more." I absolutely love this! Look back at your life, all those moments where you shed tears, those minutes where you felt so much pain you thought you'd break and scatter. You survived those. You can and will do it again.

In the military, you are a "boot" until you deploy. Once you've seen some action you become "salty" and are no longer an inexperienced boot. You are battle tested and ready. I survived drug addiction and marginalization. I fought with spirits of low self-esteem and insecurity and eventually won. I have survived every battle of my life, both physical and spiritual and so have you. With our experiences we gain wisdom. The only question remaining is: What do we do with it?

As you have read my story, it is my hope that I have encouraged you to realize the power that God has given you to overcome every obstacle, mountain and seemingly insurmountable challenge confronting you now or in the future. There are some of you reading this who have experienced failure in all walks of life, marriage, business relationships, parenting, etc. and it seems that everything you put your hand to has faltered. I not only want to encourage you, but I speak deliverance from the shackles, of mental, spiritual and emotional stagnation. I challenge you to change your mind and take on the mind of Christ. Identify with who God our Father says that you are. When this happens, you will see the chains that weighed you down and had you bound begin to fall off. If I can deposit anything into you through this chapter, I say to you, "Always be open to God's Voice." It is in His voice and the leading of His Holy Spirit that you will find peace and direction for the next phase of your life as you connect to your ordained destiny and purpose.t that time, your talents and giftings will rise like the morning sun. Remember, Jesus said in His Word, *I have told you these things, so that in me you may have peace. In this world you will have trouble, but take heart! I have overcome the world* (John 16:33, NIV).

~Dedication~

The men I have mentioned below have impacted my life tremendously in becoming the man I am today:

Apostle Arturo Skinner, Pastor and Spiritual Dad

Sherwood Johnson, Step Grandfather

Pastor Jeffries, Pastor

Bishop Wayne Johnson, Friend

Pastor Homer Green, Friend/Pastor

Bishop Phyromn Gilmer, Friend

Deacon Michael Gramble, Friend/Counselor

Dr. Calvin Ellison, Friend

Biography of Cameron Hall

Cameron Hall is a graduate of the University of South Alabama, (USA) with a Bachelor's degree in Marketing Management. While attending USA, Cameron served as the Vice President of Finance for The American Marketing Association and was an active member of The African American Student Association (AASA). A Montgomery, Alabama native, Cameron was heavily involved in church and in his community.

Mr. Hall is an emerging entrepreneur and business owner; overseeing the marketing management unit for "Plugged In." apps created by Jesse Bryant and Byruh Bryant and part owner of "More than Conquerors Inc.," (MTC), founded in Mobile, Alabama along with fellow business partners, Jarrod Cunningham, Kenji Westbrook, Kevin Engles, and Joshua Brown. His prayer is to inspire the next man to always follow their dreams and always remember that through Christ anything imaginable is possible. By submitting ourselves to the will of God, He will open many doors that the enemy tries to close. Remaining a good steward in Christ, God will always bring light to darkness.

Personal Profile

Key Words

Power, Energy, Overcoming, Pain, Visionary, Tongue

Favorite Quote

"If you can't buy it twice, don't buy it." ~Jay Z

"I am the master of my fate and captain of my soul." ~Invictus by William Ernest Henley

Values

Empowering Others, Power of God, Believing, Family, Networking, Team, Power of the Tongue, Being Fearless

Marketable Skills

Branding, Business Savvy, Innovator, Entrepreneur, Creativity and Imagination, Analytic Skills and Numeracy, Leader

Contact Information

Email: PluggedIn.Universe.gmail.com:
Plugged In Apps
    hall_337@yahoo.com
LinkedIn.com: Cameron Hall

MY STORY

Cameron Hall

Like many young men, growing up wasn't always easy. Being primarily raised by a single mother (my queen), my journey to manhood came with many obstacles. At a young age, my parents divorced, and I didn't have the privilege of growing up with a father present in the home. Many qualities that I now possess were self-taught and mirrored by other men whom I admire. Over time, my father and I have built an amazing relationship that's unbreakable. Now, I'm honored to have a father in my life.

Growing up, I would imitate and learn from many men; developing daily life skills in multifaceted manners. I would occasionally watch BET and tune in to *The Fresh Prince of Bel Air* and a personal favorite of mine, *Martin*. Watching these shows, widened my perspective of opportunities and personal growth. Being from Alabama, my exposure to black entrepreneurship was limited; immersing myself in those shows taught me that possibilities are limitless. As a fanatic sports fan, I enjoyed and loved playing football as I learned to motivate others, discipline, and work ethic.

117

Family has always been my rock, instilling values in me that I cherish and hold strong to. Being the only male in my household, I revered the role of "Man of the House" taking on duties that has carried me throughout adulthood. In addition to the many lessons learned at home, the most important lesson taught was the value of a personal relationship with Christ. Every Sunday and Wednesday my mother would force my sister, Christie and I to go to church. It almost felt like school but we ended worship early. Admittedly, my relationship with Christ did not fully develop until adulthood where I would experience a personal relationship with God. My love for music started at an early age; watching *Drumline* and attending various HBCU football games with The Mayes' family awakened my love for music, specifically drums. The precision, rhythm, and uniformed sound of the drum caught my attention which led me to becoming the church's drummer. Praise and worship is an outward expression of thanksgiving and praise; for me, the drums were a symbol of my thanksgiving and praise to God. Oftentimes, I would be so caught up in worship that the words being sung would not resonate with me until later in life. Playing the drums, I felt as if I was the heartbeat of worship, providing rhythm and soul. Being a reserved child, music was like a second language to me and gave me a voice without words.

Matthew 11:29

29 Walk with me and work with me - watch how I do it. Learn the unforced rhythms of grace. I won't lay anything heavy or ill-fitting on you.

Start of Manhood

1 Corinthians 16:13
Be on your guard; stand firm and faith; be courageous; be strong.

Leaving the nest and going to college was by far the best move I have ever made. It allowed me to experience every emotion imaginable. I worked hard and definitely played hard, but above all I graduated. Being an African American male at a predominately white institution in the South, there were definitely pros and cons. I loved the fact I was competing with world, at least in my eyes. My desire before every test was to score above everyone and be ahead of the class. However, I had to learn making good grades will only get you so far in life. I was socialized to think that having accolades and a strong resume was the key to success, nevertheless I learned that without God in my circle accolades means nothing.

Overcoming Obstacles

Isaiah 41:10
So do not fear, for I am with you; do not be dismayed, for I am your God. I will strengthen you and help you; I will uphold you with my righteous right hand.

As men, it's in our nature to fight against any obstacles in our lives. I have personally dealt with many uncanny scenarios involving toxic relationships and misleading career choices. Some of the pain we experience is indescribable; for example: the loss of a family member or friend, and even having your toe ran over with a shopping cart. I had to realize pain is the most relatable emotion one may feel. I believe that there are many people in this world who haven't experienced unconditional love, but pain is a construct that

I believe many of us have experienced in our lives. Pain is unavoidable; however, what defines our character is the ability to overcome troubling situations. Jesus reminds us through Scripture to not be worried or fearful through unwanted situations but to remain strong.

Controlling Lust

1 Corinthians 7:8-9
"To the unmarried and the widows I say that it is good for them to remain single, as I am. But if they cannot exercise self-control, they should marry. For it is better to marry than to burn with passion."

As men, we are visual individuals and temptation often creeps up on us like a thief in the night. Gentlemen, having a plethora of women doesn't make you a man or a king. Just because you have the ability to have a lot of women in your circle doesn't mean you should fornicate prematurely. Fighting sexual temptations and having strong will power makes you a stronger man and a godly king. When we fornicate before marriage, we lose power! Such power and energy, wise men use to start businesses and build their craft. The word "No" is a powerful word; do not be fooled. Being able to redirect unclean energy to passion and goals creates vivid dreams. Remember, waiting for your future wife and being loyal to your wife is an honor in God's eyes.

Speak it and Write it Down

Habakkuk 2:2

2 And the Lord answered me, and said, write the vision, and make it plain upon tables, that he may run that readeth it.

As men it is very important to have a solid approach when forming a vision. Being a visionary requires the mind to be calm and at peace so the Lord can speak to you clearer. Many factors such as, alcohol and drugs, can cloud the mind and lead to wrong decisions. As the Lord begins to speak, it is very important to write down what has been spoken to you. The ability to write down the visions are just as powerful as the vision itself. Likewise, what is written must be extremely specific and precise to what one desires. We as Christians dream to acquire more in the natural. We have our hearts set for an increase in our careers, companionship, and preferable lifestyle. God would literally give everything we desire if we are specific in our writing. The second part of the Scripture says, *Make it plain upon tables, that he may run that readeth it.* If one desires to work on the top floor of their own company overlooking a beautiful downtown scene or adjacent to water, God instructs us to be that specific. We cannot be lazy with the specifics because what is written God will bless the believer with it.

<u>Power of the Tongue</u>

Proverbs 18:21
21 The tongue has the power of life and death,
and those who love it will eat its fruit.

Gentlemen, what we say and the energy we put behind the words we use to communicate is extremely powerful. It is important to remember that the tongue carries weight and is the most powerful muscle in the body. Our words are like invisible shields and staffs; the shield helps to protect our family from the enemy by casting out unseen darkness by calling on the name of Jesus.

Using our tongues as a staff speaks life into the atmosphere by standing in agreement with Jesus. "The tongue has the power of life and death," which is true. Accordingly, one should be mindful of what they say and the intentions surrounding what is said.

~Dedication~

I dedicate this page to the individuals who have inspired me through my journey to manhood. I would personally like to say "thank you" to my mother, Cathy Hall (my Queen) and my sister, Christie Hall who have always been in my corner; they are my heartbeat. Secondly, my father, Cleophious Hall and my uncle, Willie Henry Jackson; thank you for showing me what it takes to be a man. The list below are other men who played a pivotal role to my road to manhood:

Benjamin Thomas, Oakridge, Tennessee

Dr. Terry Thomas, Raleigh, North Carolina

Daryl Thomas, Knoxville, Tennessee

Tony Thomas, Alpharetta, Georgia

Gregory Goodwin, Hurtsboro, Alabama

Roger Furman, Southfield, Michigan

Clyde Whetstone, Goodwater, Alabama

Jather Whetstone, Goodwater, Alabama

Coley Whetstone, Jr., Goodwater, Alabama

Darryl Mayes, Montgomery, Alabama

Darrly Sinkfield, Montgomery, Alabama

Patrick Buford, Huntsville, Alabama

Michael Woodham, Lorton, Virginia

Alton Jackson, Boston, Massachusetts

Jonathan Thomas, Lexington, Kentucky

Dr. Alvin Williams, Mobile, Alabama

If I miss someone, please do not charge it to my heart.

Biography of Tony Jamal Lee

Tony Jamal Lee is the Founder and Director of Afrikan Unity Initiative, Inc., a community and economic development nonprofit organization focused on promoting economic unity among all people of Afrikan descent. Jamal began hosting the Afrikan Diaspora Dialogue Series, the flagship of Afrikan Unity Initiative and our vessel used to help spread the mission of unity among people of Afrikan descent. The series began at Atlanta Metropolitan College in 2008. It was then taken to Georgia State University in conjunction with the Sankofa Society. After years of hosting the event on college campuses, it was time to open the event to the broader community which inspired the creation of Afrikan Unity Initiative. Now the program is free from collegiate affiliation and is open to the public. The goal of this program is to inform and educate people of Afrikan descent of the intentional divisive methods that continue to separate us to this day. We believe that together we can work as a collective to help solve the problems plaguing Afrikans globally. The Afrikan Diaspora Dialogue has been expanded into a series with the following subtitles: Bridging the Gap, Black2Love™, and Black2Health™. The series will be hosted three times a year with each installment being done once.

125

BLACK2LOVE™

The Afrikan Diaspora Dialogue: Black2Love™ installment focuses on the commitment it takes to seek Afrikan liberation and unity globally. This particular discussion focuses on the unifying power of love, and how it is a necessary component of any effort toward unity. We discuss how some people become arrogant and pompous once they attain a bit of Afrikan consciousness. This is not love and instead the person who knows should venture to teach those who are unknowing. It is the beautiful burden of those who gain knowledge to pass it forward in order to empower others to grow.

He envisions this discussion to serve as a catalyst to action in the communities of Afrikans. His hope is to travel to different places in the Diaspora to host this event and stream the event live over the internet for others to view. Through the streaming there is also a hope for an interactive internet experience where online viewers could join the dialogue through submitting questions via Twitter, Facebook, Google, etc. and we will address those questions and comments live during the discussion.

He is originally from Atlanta, Georgia and has dedicated his work to building communities similar to that in which he was raised. Jamal Lee served as an AmeriCorps volunteer from 2010-2013 working in youth and educational development programs in the Atlanta area. He went on to serve as a Peace Corps volunteer in Guinea, West Africa. He served as a youth community development facilitator. He was assigned to Siguiri, a village located in the Haute region. While competency in French is common among the educated population of Siguiri, Malinke/Bambara is preferred at home, in the marketplace, and in business in general. Tony Jamal Lee worked with the youth organization CECOJE and in close collaboration with local community groups, schools, as well as the surrounding population to expand and improve public health techniques, environmental stewardship activities, and natural resources management. Working alongside community partners, he exchanged innovative ideas and knowledge, directed several community projects, and facilitated trainings, focusing his efforts in the following areas:

- Jamal created hosted a series of nutrition trainings with school children ranging from the ages of 15-24. He trained over 60 youth on how to create nutritious and balanced meals affordably. He also covered when and why it is important to practice good hygiene. The three major food groups as taught in the Guinean school curriculum were covered and students engaged in creating examples of balanced meals.

- Jamal hosted a series of hand washing trainings with school children ranging from the ages of 9-15. He trained over 20 youth on how proper hand-washing techniques. He also covered when and why it is important to practice good hygiene. Children learned and actively participated in interactive games and classroom activities. Mr. Lee taught about the risks associated with not practicing good hygiene as well.

- Jamal participated in various information sessions encouraging youth to practice safe sex. The details of how HIV/AIDS is transmitted were topics of discussion as well as the importance of getting tested before marriage. The sessions were in collaboration with the youth organization CECOJE. The peer-educators of the CECOJE performed skits and other interactive learning tools.

- Jamal in collaboration with the peer-educators at CECOJE organized and participated in two quarterly information sessions advocating the prevention of pre-mature marriage of young girls. Mr. Lee stressed to a classroom of 40 young boys and girls the importance of equal education and job availability between the sexes. He also encouraged the youth to share the information they had received to their friends and family. Jamal, along with his counterpart Toumany Kouyate and the per-educators at CECOJE, organized information sessions for mothers and young girls to help with the prevention of female circumcision. Twenty-two mothers and from the greater Siguiri area were present receiving information from doctors of the local hospital on the dangers of female circumcision. Mr. Lee co-facilitated sessions on future planning and female careers.

- He hosted a series of informational sessions on malaria targeting youth visiting the local health center. He presented information on malaria transmission and bed net use using trivia, relay races and classroom sessions to approximately 100 adolescents. Mr. Lee also participated in Malaria themed soccer games to promote youth and community awareness.
- He hosted a voluntary English course Monday-Friday for community members interested in learning English. He taught on average a group of 10 consistent students. He taught the basics of sentence structure, greetings, verb conjugation, and the alphabet to his novice level pupils.

Jamal achieved an advanced level of competency in French during his service. He effectively used French to communicate in his work with community partners. In addition, he learned basic Malinke/Bambara, in which he communicated information pertinent to daily life with community members who possessed little or no ability in French.

Jamal has also lived and served in Haiti, Peru, and the Philippines doing work servicing people of Afrikan descent; continuing to build bridges throughout the Afrikan Diaspora. You can learn more about the work of Jamal Lee and AJamal Leety Initiative, Inc. at www.afrikanunity.us

Personal Profile

Key Words

Inspire, Empower, Lead

Favorite Quote

"I have not found a problem that is insurmountable with the wisdom of the elders and the energy of the youth!" ~Dr. Adelaide Sanford

Values

Building Bridges, Creating leaders, Taking Initiative

Marketable Skill

Public Speaking, Organizing, Leading, Networking

Contact Information

Email: jamal_lee@afrikanunity.us
Website: www.afrikanunity.us
LinkedIn.com: Tony Jamal Lee
Facebook: facebook.com/AfrikanUnity

MANHOOD THROUGH SERVICE

Tony Jamal Lee

Passion is the driving force that inspires great leaders to accomplish fantastic feats. I, Tony Jamal Lee, have multiple inspirational passions that insure a successful future. I have a great love for my community and for the progression of African descendants globally. I understand that the roots of many of the issues plaguing the African people across the Diaspora are psychologically driven. It is my desire to grasp the concepts within the field of psychology to help my people return to their position of honor as in ancient Africa prior to colonialism. The educating of people of all ages is a top priority to me. My appetite for learning as well as educating is immeasurable.

I have dedicated my entire life to the pursuit of educating people and the attainment of social equality. Ronald McNair is a hero of mine and to many of the youth in the Atlanta area simply by knowing of him through the many schools named in his honor. The knowledge of his life and, who he was as a person has really encouraged me in my pursuit of higher education. Coming from a similar background growing up in an Atlanta housing project, the knowledge of another

130

African-American male achieving such great triumphs continuously pushes me to surpass my educational heights. It is also a key element to my passion for service and development in underrepresented communities not unlike the one in which I was raised. I am well aware that my success thus far is greatly owed to those educators who took the time to nourish their students. I wish to pay my debt forward by providing the same care and quality learning to the next generation. The youth need a sign of hope. This is especially true among those in underserved communities and developing nations. I hope to serve as that glimmer of possibility along with the host of ancestors who came before me.

I understand that as a Black man I am seen as a threat just by virtue of being. There are a plethora of examples of this being the case throughout the history of our time in the United States. It is our responsibility to be aware of our surroundings to assist in the further advancement of our people. The absence of the Black father is not a mistake. Young men growing up without a clear example of what their role is as a man has allowed the perpetuation of false narratives to be accepted as manhood. I was fortunate to not only have my father present in my life, but also, I had a very active grandfather. I have so much appreciation for their presence as I look back over the lessons they taught. They taught me about the selflessness of manhood. I was taught by the example of two men who worked tirelessly to provide for their families and asked for very little in return. Real work is not always honored in real time. Men have to be secure enough to not always get the credit that is due to them. I take these lessons and carry them into the work that I do. This mentality makes me a better leader, husband, teacher, and community organizer today. I work to see that the young men who I encounter through my passion see an example of what a man is and by proxy change the image of Black manhood. My father grew up without his and was determined to do the exact opposite. His

131

inspiration for being there for my brother and I was giving what he had never received. The family is at the core of every community, ethnicity, and nation. The security of Afrikan Unity is the replenishment of the Black family unit. The man must know his value. This is best done early, but it is not impossible to assist our young brothers who have been misled. Those of us who know have to carry the beautiful burden of mentoring and sharing the information to which we have been given access.

I have observed that the most effective method of continuously oppressing a group of people is to control their access to education. Intellectual freedom has been a major focus throughout the Black freedom struggle from the time of enslavement to the present. In the past, there were overt restrictions that prevented people of African descent from increasing their knowledge in any form (Stewart M., 1833; Walker, 1828). This proves that those who were sanctioning these laws and policies understood that the greatest threat to their suppressive power was intellect. African people were always aware of this fact, which led them to establish alternative forms of attaining knowledge when being denied access to those of the European (Hilliard, 1995; Marable, 2000). The approach to educational bondage has now become covert which makes the detection of it more difficult. This also creates an issue for those attempting to resist the current education system because of the ambiguity of the disparities. The oppression is more systematically based and has been embedded deeply into the pedagogy of the teachers (Love & Kruger, 2005; Perlstein, 2002; Rodriguez, 1996). Many of the teachers themselves have no idea that their approach to teaching is culturally biased against non-European peoples (Rogers, 1957; Woodson, 1933).

I have had the opportunity to be an educator serving with AmeriCorps, Peace Corps, and through founding my organization Afrikan Unity Initiative, Inc. These various experiences have provided the means through which effective change can take place in the areas and communities that are in the most immediate need. Many of the students who I have had the pleasure to serve had unique home experiences and their education should be centered on these factors, or at least acknowledge the strong impact they have on the students. Culture is the basis upon which all information is filtered. This is a necessary factor to understand when attempting to educate anyone. History shows a deliberate attack against and marginalization of African culture during the enslavement era and in its aftermath. Much of this was executed through deteriorating the image of Africa, and pseudo-teachings of inherent inferiority within people of African descent. With this knowledge, it is considerably understandable why there may be academic struggles with this population. According to Carter G. Woodson (1933), mental oppression is much more treacherous than physical bondage. Within the confines of psychological conditioning, a person can be taught to favor ideas that are counterproductive to their survival (Hilliard, 1997; Woodson, 1933; X & Haley, 1964). The literature chosen helps to establish the connection of how this history influences the present aptitude contained by students of African descent within the confines of an education that offers little to no cultural significance.

There are various learning styles that are present in a group of students. Some differences fluctuate on an individual basis, but many are culturally grounded. Systematically neglecting cultural differences in learning makes academic achievement problematic for those being denied ethnic substance (Hilliard, 1995; Perlstein, 2002; Stewart, Stewart, & Simons, 2007; Rodriguez, 1996). Studies have been done regarding how they approach mathematics, which resulted in the researchers identifying that analytical methods did not function well; however, holistic tactics were successful in developing comprehension (Malloy & Jones, 1998; Martin, 2007). Holistic methodologies speak to an Afrocentric form of educating. Many of the students that I have worked with respond better to encouragement and positive reinforcement policies while teaching rather than being threatened with unfavorable grades. This shows that culturally relevant pedagogy goes beyond pure content, but it extends to the ways in which the material is presented (Hilliard, 1997; Hilliard, 1995; Malloy & Jones, 1998; Martin, 2007; Perlstein, 2002; Rodriguez, 1996). Teachers must become conscious of the importance of what and how they teach youth of all cultures. There must be a feeling of personal responsibility in educators of African descent to prevent the destruction of the minds of African peoples.

As a product of a low-income community, I had become weary of organizations coming with their "sympathy campaigns." Many have good intentions and truly mean to help; however, sympathy has an inherent connotation and outlook of superiority. This then separates those who attempt to assist from the people in need. Having this background knowledge, I have been able to build relationships with my students and members of the communities in which I work in order to show sincere empathetic intentions. An attempt to help without an understanding of the issues from the roots and without the input of the people to which the help is intended is in vain. I have been trained to emphasize empathy and how to differentiate it from sympathy. I have gained many skills and life lessons during my many years as an educator and am exceedingly appreciative of them all. I just hope that I can give to those I encounter as much as I receive from it in order to live out true reciprocity in my work.

There is a definite sense of lethargy among many instructors at the schools where I have been placed during my time as a teacher. This can be attributed to frustration with a broken education system and a population of students that have interest in seemingly anything except their education. The first rationale mentioned is a systematic battle, but the latter can be resolved through medication of the pedagogy (Perlstein, 2002; Rodriguez, 1996). Students are well aware of the disillusionment of the teachers, which separates them further from the hunger that was felt by their ancestors during enslavement. Children also know when they are not being treated fairly and whether or not they can eloquently express it. Urban youth (especially those of African descent) are approached many times as if they are inherently inferior to other peoples (Love & Kruger, 2005; Luster & McAdoo, 1994; Morris, 2004; Stewart, Stewart, & Simons, 2007). The research shows that the self-fulfilling prophesy is positively correlated to student achievement particularly when the expectations are negative (Jenkins, 2006; Love & Kruger, 2005; Morris, 2004). Not only does this affect the youth as they matriculate through school, but also has a lasting effect on the productivity of the ethnic group in society. When there are not as many skilled and educated people from one ethnicity in the work force, it has detrimental consequences for the communities in which they reside. The inferiority complex has generational results.

Within the context of the previous points it is apparent how and why students of African descent are disheartened by the thought of school. The prejudiced system of education under which they are being educated can be considered mental warfare (Jenkins, 2006; Morris, 2004; Luster & McAdoo, 1994; Stewart, Stewart, & Simons, 2007). The oppressive frame of education can and will lead to the eventual destruction of the Black community in America. There must be a conscious and intentional resistance movement geared toward students of African descent understanding the power they gain through the attainment and the application of knowledge. A clear and continuous introduction of African and African American history would show the students just how significant this battle is to the present and their future (Hilliard, 1997; Jenkins, 2006; Perlstein, 2002; Rodriguez, 1996; Woodson, 1933). There also must be willingness for teachers to battle on behalf of the students against some of the mindless policies passed by the American education system. Students need to feel as if the adults around them are their advocates and not the enemy.

My years of service have shown me how to effectively advocate for underrepresented youth and communities which is a large part of the work I do. I owe much to the training received through the many service-oriented programs I with which I have been involved and am grateful to have all of the connections and experiences gained during service. My upbringing in connection with this service has informed how I work with those who are impoverished as I once was. I now know how I can use my life's obstacles to positively influence others.

I am founder of Afrikan Unity Initiative, Inc. We are a community development non-profit organization focused on promoting economic unity among all people of Afrikan descent. We are an organization catered toward creating a better world for Afrikans and all people through interactive service and education. We are called an initiative because the word exemplifies proactivity, which is required when fighting injustice. Our model of empowering people to be the leaders they seek is attributed to Ella Baker and her participatory democracy methodology. Our initiatives are designed to work in any place around the globe in order to help people of Afrikan descent worldwide. In order to eradicate the apathy of the people empathy must be reestablished within the Afrikan community. People must understand that they are the leader who they are awaiting. The Fundi Effect makes every community member responsible for the desired change. The Fundi Effect is a method of activism that is capable of being applied inter-generationally and can address the reactionary manner with which injustice is dealt in attempts at social movements at present. In the current system of individualism and reactionary activism, The Fundi Effect has the ability to penetrate this listless generation. Social injustices are bound to become more apparent and overt if these unorganized and languid efforts persist. The best way for these methods to be applied would be for an information transfer from the Ivory Tower to the street to occur. Baker is no longer around to teach these methods, and the access to her work is presently not as available to everyday people as it should. The divide between scholars and lay people must be broken. A focus on youth leadership development is also an intricate piece of this being realized. I do not believe that education has to be confined to the classroom.

~Dedication~

Willie S. Killings

Antonio Lamar Lee

Edwin Jerome Young Jr.

Jeffery Dinkins

Richard Flynn

Deron Cloud

Rob West

Biography of Apostle Kevin Legette, Sr.

Apostle Kevin Legette, Sr. is an apostle, husband, and father. He began ministering the Gospel of Jesus Christ at 15 years of age. He ministered the Word of God as well as served as a musician. He served faithfully in the ministry under the tutelage of his uncle Bishop Liston Page, Greater Highway Fellowship. He was the Bishop, Pastor, and Founder of My Father's House International Outreach Ministries in Columbus, Georgia, in which he shepherded for 15 years. Apostle Legette knew that Father God had called him to a greater work and after joining in marriage to Apostle Andrea Zoe Legette in 2016, he accepted his call to the Apostleship.

Chosen, anointed, and destined, Apostle Kevin and Zoe Legette are a powerful couple with a Kingdom message. While winning souls, their sole purpose is to introduce, to unlock, to empower, to equip, and to train the called of God.

They have ministered to many and have established *Kingdom Works International Ministries (Conyers, GA), Transformation Cathedral Columbus (Columbus, GA), Transformation Cathedral (Conyers, GA) and Transformation Cathedral (Tifton, GA).*

Together they have five children, two grandchildren, and several spiritual sons and daughters. Christ IS their life and Kingdom Authority IS their portion!

Personal Profile

Key Words

Invest, Creative, Supernatural, Experience, Increase, Favor

Favorite Quote

"The thing that gets us into trouble is the same thing that gets us out of trouble: A Decision."

Values

Relationships, Adventurous, Wisdom and Practical Living

Marketable Skills

Public Speaking, Administration, Transportation, Musician, Media, Organizing, Leading

Contact Information

Email: mfhcol1@aol.com

Facebook: facebook.com/bishoplegette1

THE LIFE OF A SIMILAR SON

Apostle Kevin Legette, Sr.

I 'll start out writing about a son in the Bible who is so familiar to those in the church arena. As I have read the story so many times, even ministering it a time or two, I saw that I myself was on the same path as this son.

Let me start out by quoting a passage of Scripture that is extremely vital to all of us as men, both young and old. *Now that I say, that the heir, as long as he is a child, differeth nothing from a servant, though he be lord of all; but is under tutors and governors until the time appointed of the father* (Galatians 4:1-2, KJV). My dear brothers, this is very important to all of us, because it speaks to the importance of having a strong and active father in our lives, both boys and girls. I say active because there are a lot of fathers in their children's lives, but not active in the sense of demonstrating the true characteristics of a father.

The father represents headship, because he has stored up an inheritance for his son. I believe that there is something in life stored up for us all to help us achieve all that we need for success in life. The father embodies leadership because he has set in place governors and tutors to prepare his son for the future. The father also represents patience because he has set a time guide for his son to reach a level of maturity; not to control his son, but to stress the importance of his son maturing in a timely manner. We know that a chronological age is not the standard for maturity; rather, it's all about the mindset. If your mind is channeled in the right direction at an early age, you can do many incredible things in life. As for me, I didn't have that father figure at an early age. Therefore, a lot of major decisions didn't get the attention that they desperately needed.

This son in the Bible had a father in his life who was very active, who provided headship, leadership, and patience, but the son decided to ignore the process of maturing and set out to take control of his life. Because he chose to shorten his maturing process, we see he experienced some unnecessary (due to his decisions), yet necessary (to bring him to submission) hardships. One, the son was unable to make the right connections in life. As the Scripture makes us aware of, *"Be not deceived: evil communications corrupt good manners"* (1 Corinthians 15:33, KJV). This son wanted his inheritance too soon. When you are not mentally ready to handle abundance, abundance has a way of handling you. As we see with this son, he began to waste his substance with riotous living.

Discipline, my brothers, is one of the characteristics that comes with the maturing process. What I want you to focus on at this point is, as soon as he gets his portion, he decided to break away from the very thing that was supporting, guiding, giving identity, strengthening, imparting, and maturing him. It is very important to cherish the moments you have in your early years when there is someone imparting into your life. As a young man with substance, but not the mental maturity he needed, he shows us the path that life will place you on as a result of not appreciating all the valuable people who tried to impact his life. There is nothing more important in life than having the wisdom and necessary tools you need to get through life. Life has a way of making you or breaking you.

Notice the process of not having a mature and stable mind. The son wasted his substance in so many lascivious (uncontrollable) ways that caused him to end up with nothing, as if he never had anything or anyone in his life at all. Now, here comes one of those unforeseen moments in life that he had no control over. A famine hits and devastates his life and all those around him. Another thing you must understand is that money does give you options, but when you operate without a mature and stable mind, you end up with no money and when all your money is gone, you have no options. Now life is dictating to this young man how he should, where he should, and who he should live with. It doesn't always work in your favor when life is calling the shots. He has abandoned the government of his father, so now he has to submit to another government that he is not familiar with; the government of other people who do not have his best interest at heart. He is forced to take a job he doesn't like and is beneath his background of where he comes from, because he has no options. He is developing an appetite, a desire for what was for animals to feed off of. We tend to gravitate to stuff that we are surrounded by on a day-to-day basis.

One thing I can celebrate about this young man is that he is not lazy, but when you don't take advantage of an education, you can't make the best career choices in life. This story does not end tragic as most of our lives do: on drugs, multiple babies, a dead-end job, no money;

where options are very limited. The son does something that I think we all should take a greater look at. We may not all have had the benefit of having someone beneficial in our upbringing, but there is, I believe, in all of us the unction to get up from where we are and live. It was his desire to live by another standard better than the option life chose for him. He looked deep inside himself and remembered where his source of strength, power, identity, discipline, patience, order, and mental maturity came from and decided to reconnect. When he reconnected to the government of his father, his father put on him a robe, a ring, and slippers. Wow, what an outfit for success! The robe of righteousness, a ring of authority, and slippers that pointed him in the right direction.

Well, you may say, "I didn't have a father" and that may be true, but I believe somewhere in your life, there may have been some very important people who came across your path to positively impact your life somehow. All I ask is that you dig like this son, deep inside, and remember some of the things that they taught you and get up from where you are and begin to live! If you did not have a father figure, mentor, or someone who was a voice of wisdom, don't let that stop you! Just begin to recognize the important people who *will* cross your path. Cherish every nugget they drop on you that will take you where you need to go in life.

I said all of that to say this...that my life was parallel to this son in so many ways because I had no father figure to help in those tender years of molding and shaping. A lot of what I learned came from media, various friends, and family members whom I thought were smart and wise. So many years later, I learned that what information I had obtained from these sources was so off track and that it caused me to waste a lot of precious years. Being left up to my own intellect, major decisions that I deemed to be important were not that important at all. I made a lot of unnecessary things and people necessary that I shouldn't have. Furthermore, being in the church, I thought, would make my life work for me. Not! I came to find out that so many people in the church were not who they portrayed themselves to be. When the Scripture says "beware of wolves in sheep's' clothing," this is so very true. It wasn't until I found some true to the faith people that I realized there was another "church" inside the "church" that was being presented. The real Church or Body of Christ is where I found that information that I needed to make my life work according to the Kingdom. All my bad decisions, wrong turns, wrong company, being in places I should have never been, and consuming stuff that I should have never consumed, I was able to eliminate from my life.

Like the son described in the Bible, I too had come to myself and made a decision. It's funny when you look at it. The same thing that put my life in such an uproar was the same thing that turned it around...a decision! The son made a decision to get up from where he was and put things back in their proper perspective. It started with reconnecting with his father that pointed his new life in the right direction. Just like this son, I myself did the same thing. Although, I didn't have my father in my life, I found, recognized, and attached myself to father figures and submitted myself to their knowledge. There, I realized the turn I so desperately needed for the life I desired.

I don't have to tell you that it wasn't material things I needed to make my life work. What I needed to make my life work was peace of mind, happiness within myself, happy *with* myself, and being able to love myself more than anything in the world. It is in this place where you begin to build and enjoy life.

Let someone who has the ability to impact and impart into you help you shape your life, so that one day, not only will you be able to be an example in life, but also *be* an example of life. You will be able to do the same thing for someone else who has a similar life as yours.

~Dedication~

Todd Longstreth, Snellville, GA

Melvin Stringer, Conyers, GA

Aaron Richmond, Columbus, GA

Vincent Lynch, Conyers, GA

Onigh McMoore, Conyers, GA

Kevin Legette, Jr., Conyers, GA

Brandon Allen, Conyers, GA

Biography of Jerome K. Miller

Jerome K. Miller, 24 years of age, was born in Savannah, Georgia to Tara L. Miller as her only child. He currently resides in Atlanta, Georgia. He's a first-generation college student, community activist, mentor to young men, actor, and investor. He currently attends Georgia State University as an undergraduate student pursuing his degree in Interdisciplinary Studies with a major in Social Entrepreneurship and a concentration in Global Issues. His expected graduation date is May 2020. After graduation, his plan is to pursue a MIB (Master's in International Business) and curate his own nonprofit.

Jerome, has expertise in Finance & Managerial issues; as he has been a part of a study abroad to Dubai and the UAE as well as expertise in the Economic & Environment of Business in South Africa as the atlas student of the group. There, he consulted individuals of South Africa on how to start a business and build traction. Jerome, is a student ambassador at LaunchGSU, which is an incubator space for aspiring entrepreneurs who want to start a business or continue working on an existing one, or curate a start-up. He's an ambassador of CASA (Center for the Advancement of Students & Alumni) at Georgia State University, a member of the leadership program at Georgia State University, vice president of a nonprofit organization called Greatest MINDS, brand ambassador at the HJ Russell Center for Innovation & Entrepreneurship, newly integrated member of the Atlanta Men's Dinner Group, and has affiliations with CUMU (Coalition of Urban & Metropolitan Universities). In October 2019 as part of his affiliations with CUMU, he spoke on a panel about his upbringings, empowering young individuals to not give up despite their surrounding circumstances and making it from his hometown. In his downtime, whenever that may permit itself, Jerome has a fetish for reading, listening to Jazz music, meditation, and mentoring young men.

Personal Profile

Key Words
Elegant, Immaculate, Distinguished, Knowledge, Resiliency

Favorite Quote
"Continue to be a strong black king, not a strong black man."

Values
Loyalty, Hard work, Dedication, Meaningful & Effective Relationships, Empowering Others

Marketable Skills
Networking, Public Speaking, Effective Communicator, Leading, Thinking Outside of the Box

Contact Information
Email: Jerome.kmiller95@gmail.com
LinkedIn.com: Jerome Miller
Facebook: facebook.com/JeromeMiller

WHERE ART THOU KINGS?

Jerome K. Miller

In a world where the high power is recognized as the Lord of Lords and King of Kings, it's exemplified since the beginning of time the value of what the term, *king* embodies. The term *king*, according to the Merriam-Webster dictionary, is defined *as a male monarch of a major territorial unit and one whose position is hereditary and who rules for life.* The understanding that I take from that definition is simple. Without a king, the world and the people of the world can become discombobulated and in shambles. In order for a community, country, and the world to be able to cooperate and be on one accord there has to be a king, and one who understands his calling of being a king. First and foremost, every male that's born into this world is a king. Obviously you have to hold the monarch of being a prince first, but you should be able to draw between the lines of where I'm going with this; because here is where the problem can occur which can start an argument/debate based off of the statement I just mentioned. In order to support the statement that

I just made and be able to understand where I'm going with this, here's a distinction.

Yes, every male that's born into this world is a king, but in order for that statement to come into fruition, a man has to be able to first recognize as a young boy that he is a king and has to understand that without anyone having to inform him. In order for a man to understand his calling of being a king, he first has to understand himself, understand his strengths and weaknesses, have the courage to be able to work on his weaknesses, understand his environment and be able to recognize the root causes of the problems in his environment. But most importantly, in order to be a king, a man has to be able to understand the people and be able to accept humility. If a man doesn't understand the people and can't accept humility, then he can't lead and without leadership, you can't be a king! Being that I was born in 1995 and now today in the year 2020, I sense, understand, and know that there is a shortage of kings in our society. However, if you continue to read along and travel on this enticing journey with me, I will expound upon in four different instances the reasons on why I believe these are such the cases today.

REASON #1 – THE MOTHER WAS THE FATHER

This a tricky one, correct? This topic can spark up a great debate and propose counterarguments and an array of different types of viewpoints. I, myself, can probably somewhat disagree with this being a reasoning of why there is a shortage of kings, because of the mother being the father and why that statement may be subjective. But the content that I'm going to provide you with will prove in fact, why the statement is objective and is indeed, a reason why there's a shortage of kings. According to an article on news.gallup.com, in a household, mothers are the dominant influence and this statement has remained the same since 1951. And today, more than half of the

150

American adults polled, 53% indicated that this is indeed true. Contributing factors that play a role pertinent to why the mother has to be the father and has a larger influence when it comes to raising a boy, the father may be incarcerated or the father is too busy indulging in activities relating to the streets and enjoying the enticement of living the fast life. The father is maybe afraid to take care of his responsibilities when it comes to caring for and nurturing a young boy. The age at which the man becomes a father may range from 16 to 21 and he may feel that he hasn't yet matured. So because of that, he probably wouldn't understand how to raise a boy or he's probably having relations with other women which causes havoc and this leaves the woman whom he had the baby with to take care of the child on her own. Now, I'm not stating that a woman can't raise a boy to be a man and prepare him to be a king, but what I am stating is that the rate at which kings could be prevalent in today's society will be heightened based off of an effective foundation beginning at home in his upbringings with both the mother and father being present.

The ability to have a father in the household is very fortunate and it comes with great benefits. The father can indoctrinate and show a young boy many things, such as teaching him how to have values, morals, be able to fight through adversity, respect women and never to call them out of their name, how to work hard for what he wants in life and never ask anyone for anything, how to be head of the household and take care of his family, how to be responsible, leadership traits, how to be an asset for his community, and prepare him for society once he decides to leave from underneath his wing. If a father completes his task of these things, to name a few, then he has completed a job well done and will have raised a king. But because there's been a shortage of fathers who may be equivocal of this criterion, the duty of raising a king falls into the responsibility of the mother which may correlate to less kings being produced and the epitome of what being a king entails never being taught or learned.

REASON #2 – LACK OF UNDERSTANDING

Young boys and men just don't understand. I, at first, was going to say they are lost but that's more of an understatement. In order for a man to be a king, he has to be taught it, he has to be shown it, he has to have his eyes, ears, and mind constantly open so that they all can be watered with information and knowledge. This will propel him to grow and flourish so that he can garner an understanding of what being a king personifies. If you plant seeds from the beginning, you continuously water it; you let it get some sunshine when it's hot, you let it get some water when it rains, and you give it proper nutrients. If cared for consistently, you will have a full, grown plant. Now, apply that analogy to that of understanding the value and importance of what it means to be a king. It's the same concept and you'll get the same result. But if you don't apply this analogy or an analogy that can be somewhat similar, then a step in the process will be missing and the understanding of raising a king or the principle in general can be completely eradicated.

REASON #3 – LEADERSHIP IS LOST. WHERE IS IT?

Can you motivate a group of people? Can you be selfless? Do you have goals? Can you accept failure? Have you experienced the feeling of failure? Are you dedicated? Most importantly, is it all about you? When an individual can honestly answer those few questions, then it's inevitable that he has the ability and capability to not only lead, but be a king. The art of what I just summoned is another reason why there is a shortage of kings. A gargantuan amount of men can't answer these questions; and the reason why is because there's an extinction of black men who can't lead, who are not in the household to lead, and have never been put into position to lead because there's a lack of leaders in our communities.

Every couple of generations, you have a few leaders: Malcolm X, Martin Luther King, Jr., Theodore Roosevelt, Thomas Jefferson, Tupac Shakur, Michael Jordan, the late Kobe Bryant, the late Ermias Asghedom, Barack Obama, Shawn Carter (Jay-Z), and Herman J. Russell. The characteristic they all had in common is they each could answer the questions that I proposed in my earlier statement. They all were trendsetters. They all were strong, bold, didn't care about the perception of what other's thought, most of them were great assets to the communities, did things their way, and they all didn't fear losing. Most importantly, every person that I mentioned all faced trials and tribulations earlier on. But in order to be a king, you have to be persistent and relentless on your path and not let anything get into the way of you being great and creating a legacy.

There's a problem that arises here though; hatred, envy, and jealousy. However, I won't dwell on those three. The point that I'm trying to get across is where are the next leaders? Not leaders of this generation and the coming generation. Where are our leaders for today? Who's going to set the blueprint for the leaders of tomorrow to follow so when it's their time to lead, they'll be ready? Here's the problem on why leadership is lost and kings are not being produced. Everyone wants to be leaders, but not everyone is born one. First, you must learn how to follow and master the art of that. Then once you master that, you can be put to the test to see if you can lead. Once you figure out if you can lead, then you develop your leadership philosophy and the test shall be passed to promote you to a king.

REASON #4 – IDENTITY

What is your name? Do you understand the meaning behind your name? Where are you from? Where does your ancestors originate from; do you know? Do you understand yourself? Why was I put here? Hmmm, my brother, you were put here just like each and every one of us, to be a king and understand your royalty. In 2020, young boys and men don't grasp this concept and this is why there's a shortage of kings! Nowadays, young boys would rather be followers and gravitate to what they see and become a product to their environment, a statistic to society, and a slave to the prison system and racial world than be a king; let alone a man. Whereas men don't even understand the influence they have on young men because the man was the seed who brought the young man into this world. Eight times out of ten, whatever actions or lifestyle a boy sees his father or a man commit, he's going to follow in those footsteps and the young boy or man will never get the chance to understand his identity. The advice I can pass down to any young boy or man out there to help generate a reduction to this generational problem is to figure out why you're here and understand your purpose for being here. Next, understand and know your history so that you can comprehend the importance of the past, present, and future and learn from important public figures, so that you can have some direction on the type of future/legacy you are supposed to create, leave, and pass down to the next generation of young kings, whenever your time may come to an end. Most importantly, put on your armor, tie up your shoes, and step outside of your comfort zone and don't be afraid to do so. During this time is when, if you haven't already, you will realize your identity, understand who you are, understand your purpose in life, and figure out where you may belong in the world. This, ladies and gentlemen, is when a King is born because they have been able to identify certain aspects of life and their life as well, which is truly a feeling like no other, and can't be taken away.

Now, young man, as you may go on your journey, have a conversation with the higher power (the real King of Kings). But be brave and confident, understand the importance and reasoning on why you are here and understand your value and the power that you have within yourself. This is when the question of *Where Art Thou Kings?* shall cease.

~Dedication~

Tara Miller, Savannah, GA

Jonathan Mclaughlin, Atlanta, GA

Antonio Powell, Savannah, GA

Kalee Edwards, Savannah, GA

Ricardo Manuel, Savannah, GA

Isaiah Simmons, Atlanta, GA

George Greenidge, Boston, MA

Ermias Asghedom, Los Angeles, CA

Kobe Bryant, Los Angeles, CA

Malcolm X, Omaha, NE

Paula Huntley, Brooklyn, NY

Mourad Dakhli, Atlanta, GA

Sharon Cavusgil, Atlanta, GA

Joyce Davis, Savannah, GA

Michelle Dawkins, Springfield, MA

Biography of Pastor Tony Phillips

Pastor Tony Phillips is the senior and founding pastor of Trinity Fellowship Ministries. Called to ministry in 1991 under the leadership of the late Bishop W.L. Phillips. Pastor Phillips was ordained as an Elder in the United African American Free Will Baptist Association, where he served faithfully for 6 years. Afterwards he joined Deeper Life Church Ministries in Goldsboro, NC, under the leadership of Apostle Norbert E. Simmons where he served faithfully for 8 years. In 2001, Pastor Phillips founded Trinity Fellowship Ministries and planted the church in Wilson NC on November 12, 2006. In August 2008, Pastor Phillips joined the Full Gospel Baptist Church Fellowship under the leadership of Bishop Paul S. Morton, Sr., Presiding Bishop A.G. Mullen - State Bishop and Overseer Alphonso Smith - District Overseer. Pastor Phillips served as the 1st assistant to the Overseer for the East Central District.

Pastor Phillips is the author of one book, entitled: "My Encounters With The Third Person." Pastor Phillips has a tremendous passion for God's Word and the teaching of sound doctrine. He teaches the word with revelation and simplicity so that it is easily understood. He received his first minister training in the United American Free Will Baptist College in Kinston, NC and has devoted years of Bible study learning to build mature Christians for the kingdom of God. He is known for his spirit of humility and love for God's people.

Pastor Phillips is married to Elder Theresa Phillips. He is a devoted husband and father. Together the two of them complete an anointed duo that God is using to make a change in the lives of people. They have five wonderful children, Ricky, Jamiyan, Chermia, Dominique, and Caleb. One daughter in law, Latrice and one son in law, Brian. Seven grandchildren, Jamiya, Emery, Jade, Journi, Jude, Dawson and Canaan. Two god children, Shaketa Hudson and Chase Wilkes.

Personal Profile

Key Words
Sound, Inquisitive, Depth, Grasp, Convey

Favorite Quote
"Well done is better than well said."

Values
Love, Friendship, Teamwork, Family, Faith

Marketable Skills
Ethics, Adaptability, Speaking and Listening, Multidisciplinary

Contact Information
Email: miyajadeem@gmail.com

Facebook: Tony Phillips (Pastor Tony Phillips)

IMITATION OF MY FATHER

Pastor Tony Phillips

S ome fathering advocates say that almost every social ill faced by America's children is related to fatherlessness. Children from fatherless homes are more likely to be poor, become involved in drug and alcohol abuse, drop out of school, and suffer from health and emotional problems. Boys are more likely to become involved in crime, and girls are more likely to become pregnant as teens when a father is not present in the home. (http://fathers.com/) *And, ye fathers, provoke not your children to wrath: but bring them up in the nurture and admonition of the Lord* (Ephesians 6:4, KJV). *Train up a child in the way he should go: and when he is old, he will not depart from it* (Proverbs 22:6, KJV).

"The United States anti-narcotics campaign partnership for a drug-free America launched a commercial in July, 1987. The campaign used a televised public service announcement that featured a father confronting his son in his bedroom after finding a box containing an unspecified controlled substance and drug paraphernalia. After his father angrily asked him how he learned to use drugs, the son shouts, "You, alright.?! I learned it by watching you!" As the father recoils by realizing the error of his ways, a narrator then intones, parents who use drugs have children who use drugs." (https://en.wikipedia.org/wiki/I_learned_it_by_watching_you!)

Like father, like son, the son was an imitation of his father. *Jesus and said unto them, Verily, verily, I say unto you, The Son can do nothing of himself, but what he seeth the Father do: for what things soever he doeth, these also doeth the Son likewise. For the Father loveth the Son, and sheweth him all things that himself doeth: and he will shew him greater works than these, that ye may marvel* (John 5:19-20).

Children suffer the consequences of their parents' actions. But they can't use their father's weaknesses to free themselves of responsibility. A convicted son cannot say, "I'm not in jail because of any fault of my own, but I'm suffering for the sins of my father." The Lord told Ezekiel that just because the fathers have sinned (eaten sour grapes) doesn't mean the sons should be punished (have their teeth set on edge). Ezekiel argued that righteous children do not suffer for their parents' wickedness; nor do wicked children benefit from their parent's righteousness.

The Sovereign LORD said, "You will not repeat this proverb (excuse) in Israel any more. The life of every person belongs to me, the life of the father as well as that of the son. The person who sins is the one who will die." The son and/or the grandson is free to change once he sees and understands the consequences of his father's wickedness. (Ezekiel 18:1-4, 25-32, Commentary by Margaret Odell; https://www.workingpreacher.org/)

Have you heard about the legacy of Jimmy Walker and Jalen Rose? Jimmy Walker was a two-time NBA All-Star basketball player. Jalen Rose, is a former NBA player, 1994/ Round: 1/ Pick: 13th overall. He is also the current Sports Analyst for ESPN, and cofounder of the Jalen Rose Leadership Academy. Jimmy Walker is the biological father of Jalen Rose. Leaving Jalen's mom prior to his birth, Walker took no part in Jalen's upbringing. Jimmy Walker enjoyed the fruit of his labor and fame benefiting from healthy earnings befitting a top-round pick and an All-Star while Jeanne, Jalen's mother, struggled raising four kids. Jeanne was a single mom working at Chrysler on a small salary as a keypunch clerk to provide for her family.

"No electricity, no hot water, no heat -- at times we struggled," Rose, the youngest of Jeanne's kids, says. "We'd wake up in the morning and wash with water we heated on a hot plate. And we'd go to bed at night wearing skull caps, sweatshirts and gloves." (https://www.lipstickalley.com/threads/excellent-article-on-jalen-rose-and-his-pops.98461/)

Walker died on July, 2, 2007, at the age of 63, from complications related to lung cancer. Rose never knew Walker; never even met him. The first time Rose and Walker shared the same room was at his funeral. Rose, however, was still unable to set his eyes on the man who gave him life. Walker had been cremated. Rose learned a valuable lesson 22 years ago from the late Sam Washington, who was the director of St. Cecilia. Tired of Rose's constant goofing off in a sixth-grade class, Washington led him to the basement office. Clicking off the lights, he fed a reel into a projector and played highlights of Walker -- a solidly built shooting guard who reminded many of Oscar Robertson -- on the wall. "That's your father," he told Rose, who sat mesmerized by the footage. "You have the same potential to be very special." A few weeks after watching the film,

Rose tore open a pack of basketball cards, and guess whose image looked up at him? Walker. He slipped the card into his pocket and carried it everywhere he went. Rose began to create an alter ego to his famous father. Hearing that Walker put on shows with his basketball skills at St. Cecilia, Rose did the same. Knowing that Walker had worn No. 24, Rose flipped the script and selected No. 42. "I made a vow that one of the main things I wanted to accomplish in my life is that one day he'd know my name." It's the 1992 NCAA Tournament. The nation's most intriguing team is Michigan, which features the Fab Five -- all freshman starters, including Jalen Rose. Mission accomplished: Everyone knows his name. In 1997, Rose's second year in Indiana, the Pacers drafted Austin Croshere out of Providence. In 1999, Croshere handed Rose a piece of paper. On it was Walker's phone number. Rose picked up the phone and, after 27 years, nervously uttered the first words he had ever spoken to his father: "Can I speak to Jimmy?"

Rose told his father that he had no hard feelings, that he was happy with his life, that he knew exactly where the athleticism he was blessed with came from. Walker told his son that he had followed his career, and that he was proud of how he had developed as a player. http://www.espn.com/nba/news/story?page=Rose-Walker

Rose told this story during his interview on the Breakfast Cub radio show one morning and Charlamagne, the host said, "Thank your father for the donation. Thank him for the sperm."

Rose said, "My father wasn't there for me, but I got his DNA. I could do what he did and even better."

Men, if greatness can come from the DNA of a man, how much more the DNA of God?

Bad as you are, you know how to give good things to your children. How much more, then, will your Father in heaven give good things to those who ask him! (Matthew 7:11, GNB)

How much more, then, will the Father in heaven give the Holy Spirit to those who ask him! (Luke 11:13, GNB)

They did not become God's children by natural means, that is, by being born as the children of a human father; God himself was their Father. (John 1:13, GNB)

This holds true today. We as humans purpose in our hearts to do well toward our children, but sometimes there is some bad mixed in with the good because we are human; we are not a perfect people. Often times, the negative we impart may not be intentional as our lives are shaped by consequences and choices that we make. Just as the statistics show those who are fatherless, not by any choice of their own and for different reasons, regardless affect the lives of the children in a negative way. As I look back over my life, I can see how my life was shaped by both the positive as well as the negative things I learned from my father.

I am a third-generation pastor. My grandfather was the late, Bishop Willie E. Phillips and my father was the late Robert E. Phillips, Sr. My father pastored several churches in the United American Free Will Baptist Association and my grandfather was the Bishop. To all who didn't know my father, just look at me. I am a version of my father. I look just like him, talk like him, walk like him. I even hold my head to the side like him. As you can see, I come from a legacy of pastors and I too am a preacher and most recently founding pastor of Trinity Fellowship Ministries. I recall when I was in middle school my guidance counselor asked me, what did I want to be when I grew up. I replied, "A preacher!" My counselor was shocked, because I didn't say I wanted to be profession basketball player or football player. I believe this was one of the first imitations of my father which came through my lineage, but I also believe it was the plan of God for my life. I got it honest because all I knew was preaching the gospel. I was born into a preacher's family and not just my dad and granddad, but uncles and aunts were preachers as well. Church was a very important and large part of my upbringing. I went to Sunday school and church every Sunday. During this time, my grandfather was the pastor and my father was a deacon and a Sunday school teacher. He also sang in the church male chorus where he would often lead songs. I recall one time I led one of the songs that my dad would lead with the male chorus. While singing his song in church, I felt the Holy Spirit moving all over me. Some of the saints said I sounded just like my dad. If they only knew I purposely tried to imitate him. I wanted to be just like my dad. My dad worked at Harris Supermarket, preached the gospel, and sang in the choir, and I too wanted to do all of these things, because my dad did them. He truly was my idol.

In 1991, God called me into the ministry. I had a grand start and the Holy Spirit was present when I preached that night. I recall the night I preached my initial sermon, my father stood to give remarks. He approached the podium, opened his mouth, but couldn't say a word. He was overwhelmed with joy when he witnessed the anointed on my life. Shortly after preaching my initial sermon, my father made me the assistant pastor at of one of his churches. This was a great honor. Even then I would imitate my father while I was preaching. My mannerisms and charisma were much like his, often leaning back, standing on one leg, and thundering my voice while preaching, just like he would do. Some years later I began to find myself and my style of preaching changed; however, my older brother, still preaches much like him today.

My father loved preaching the gospel. He was at church at least three or four nights a week. He was the pastor of three different churches at one time and there was always a service, a meeting, or something going on at one of the churches. Because of his commitment to the churches he pastored, my father was away from home a lot. One of my earliest memories of this was when I tried out for little league football. I actually made the team and was chosen to be quarterback, but I never played in a single game. I got tired of being stranded after practice, not having transportation to get home. My father was at church from 7:00pm until 10:00pm most nights. There was no one to pick me up after practice to take me home, so I quit the team. This was a great disappointment to me, but all was not lost. My dad was still there for us.

I recall during my early childhood days before becoming so involved in church, my father was very involved with his children. He would take my older brother and I to work with him some days where he taught us how to stock groceries on the shelves at Harris Supermarket. But our favorite was going fishing every Thursday in Hoboken, N.C. He loved quartet singing and would also take us to the Guy Smith Stadium to enjoy the gospel singers in the summer. For Halloween, he would buy us costumes, masks, and candy. On Easter, he bought us Easter baskets and new bikes, BB guns and toys for Christmas. We'd go to the local fair and he would buy us cotton candy, candy apples, and give us money to play games. I even remember getting money from the tooth fairy. There was a time when my father was very supportive. He supported our education by paying for lunch, school fees and providing money for trips. He even bought us a puppy, which I was afraid to touch. I remember my dad escorting me to kindergarten class and then first grade. He taught us the importance of education by requiring us to do our homework, go to bed on time, and get up early and prepare for school each day. He laid a good foundation of love and support in me. He didn't have an education beyond high school, but he made sure we knew it was important for us to get more than what he had. He didn't want us to have the same struggles in life as he did.

Even though I watched my dad and received good things from his parenting, the lack of support once he began pastoring didn't have a positive effect on my life. However, when I got saved, I started going down that same path. Sometimes I was in church several nights a week. I was a part of the outreach team (street ministry) and would spend all day Saturday doing outreach, going door to door witnessing. Each Sunday we would arrive to church at 8:00am for Elders' prayer. This was a requirement at that time as I was an elder at the church. Sunday school would follow at 9:00am; then 10:00am the leaders assembled for prayer. Morning Worship was at 11:00am and often lasted until 2 pm. Every Sunday there was a 6:00pm service. I have to admit this was a long day for my family and I had young children. I found myself spending a lot of time in church with my wife and children in attendance, that I could have been spending at home with my family. When my children got old enough to participate in activities outside of church, my wife and I learned how to balance church and family. I didn't want my children to experience what I did when I tried out for football and didn't have the support that I needed to play. As a nurturing father, I supported my children. I attended all of their events whether during or after school. My wife and I made sure one of us were there, if not both. I would pick them up from practice and attend their games. I supported pageants, summer ventures, science Olympiad, cheering competitions, and chaperoned field trips. You name it; I was there. My wife and I attended parent-teacher conferences and our children were high performing academically gifted students. I was surely breaking the cycle that I had become a part of. I was able to do all of this while keeping them active in the church. They were involved in teen meetings, bible study, liturgical dance team, drill team and mime ministry. I had a rule in my house that, if you didn't praise God and participate in church, then you couldn't participate at extra-curricular activities in school. like playing sports or being a cheerleader. If you didn't stand up and clap your hands for Jesus, you couldn't play football. I supported my children spiritually, physically, and financially. As a result of my parenting, support and guidance I raised successful children. My oldest son graduated from N.C. State University with a Sociology degree. My second son is a graduate of North Carolina A&T State University with a degree in Sports Science and a minor in Recreation. My daughter graduated from UNC Chapel Hill with a degree in Communication and holds a Master's Degree in Speech and Language Pathology from East Carolina University. My next to the youngest son graduated from East Carolina University with a degree in Business Information Technology Education. My youngest son is completing his freshman year of high school and is sure to follow in their footsteps.

Most of the men in my grandfather's lineage did not graduate from high school or go to college. My father had to drop out of high school to go to work. He was raised in a family that didn't have much. My father married my mother and had six children and they struggled at times to make ends meet. I remember those hard times when the electricity was disconnected, water cut off, or car repossessed. My school wardrobe consisted of five pair of wrangler jeans, five short sleeve shirts, and a pair of inexpensive tennis shoes. My brother and I jokingly called the tennis shoes "fish heads" because the shoes were cotton with a hard bottom sole, a rubber toe and resembled a fish. The second half of the school year, my father would buy me a wind breaker jacket and a pair of boots to wear during the winter. As we grew into teenagers, my older siblings and I began to work in the tobacco fields during the summer. It was then that we were able to buy our own clothes for school. I was happy to purchase name brand clothes such as Sergio Valente jeans with the bullhead symbol, polo shirts and Adidas. You couldn't tell me anything! My dad would charge us $15 per week for rent. We grumbled about paying it, but we later understood he was teaching us responsibility and money management. Again, I allowed this experience to shape me as I raised my children. I worked hard to provide them with more than what I had. I made sure to get the top paying jobs that I could qualify for and later went on to obtain my Commercial Driver's License to make more money to provide an even better lifestyle for my family. My children wore name brand clothes that I purchased and were able to take family trips and summer vacations. I learned from my father and was able to do more for my children. They worked at their own choosing but never because they had to and I never required them to pay rent while they lived in my house. It was my responsibility to take care of them and I wanted them to enjoy liberties that I never did.

My father went home to be with the Lord in July 1991. He left us a legacy; not of money, but of faith, integrity, good worth ethics, faithfulness, and humility. I would describe my father as a good man, faithful husband, provider for his children and a preacher of righteousness. He instilled those things in me. I learned them from watching him. Like Jalen Rose, I have my father's DNA. His legacy continues in the earth today through me as I wear the Phillips name with pride. I have learned from my father's mistakes as well as his successes. As men we must learn how to turn negatives into positives. We can't throw the negatives away or pretend they never happened because they help shape us into the men we are today. However, we can take that negative and make a promise to ourselves not to do the same thing, allow it to be a learning experience. Instead of allowing the negative to form a generational curse like that of the lack of education in my family we can be the one to break the generational curse. I knew the importance of education not because I had one but because I didn't have one. And I refused to allow my children to follow down that path. I wanted more for them so I made sure to support them and instill educational values in them. The memory of not having the support of my father to play sports is a negative memory of my childhood but I didn't allow it to make me bitter. I allowed it to make me better. I made sure I was there for my children to give them an opportunity to play sports and other extra-curricular activities of interest. Those negatives turned to positives in my life and have trickled down to my children and have helped shape my sons to be loving, supportive fathers who take care of their children. I will exceed my father him as a successor. I will live longer. I will be a better man. I will do more and I will go further. In fact, I have already achieved several of these things.

Unlike Jimmy Walker, my father wasn't a star player on the court living a lavish life style while his family struggled to make ends meet, but he (my father) supported his family. I believe he did the best with what he had. And while his being good to his children were simple things like going fishing or taking us to work with him, those things are treasured today. Most importantly he left me something that money nor fame could buy and that was a legacy of faith in God. The God who gives the best gift to his children. And just like the young man cloned in the commercial who learned how to do drugs by watching his father, I learned how to have faith in God by watching my father. This priceless gift makes up for all the other things that money couldn't buy or maybe he didn't have the time to share. Father's need to realize whether absent or present you are the first man your son will ever see and what you do will leave an impression on his life. Make every effort that it is a positive impression that your son will be glad to imitate.

~Dedication~

Jamiyan Phillips, Greenville NC

Dominique Phillips, Winterville, NC

Ricky Phillips, Cary, NC

Joseph Moore, Farmville, NC

Terry Morris, Grifton, NC

Ray Williams, Goldsboro, NC

Harry Davis, Wilson, NC

Trey Sheppard, Greenville, NC

Boris Perry, Rocky Mount, NC

James Phillips, Winterville, NC

Doug Davis, Greenville, NC

Jeffrey Winbush, Goldsboro, NC

Brian Spruill, Knightdale, NC

Donald Evans, Wilson, NC

Boris Phillips, Greenville, NC

Biography of Tod Rose

Tod Rose, *entrepreneur, author*, and *businessman*, are three words that describe what Tod Sterling Rose does. But who he is would be encompassed by the words *father, husband* and *overall student of life*.

Rose is a 1997 graduate of the historic Morris Brown College in Atlanta, Georgia where he earned a bachelor's degree in Journalism. As an entrepreneur and businessman, Rose owns T.S. Rose Enterprises, LLC which is comprised of two distinct, yet related, businesses: copycontentarticles.com and budgetsearchpro.com. Through these entities, he employs his expert internet marketing skills to help other entrepreneurs' market and grow their businesses online and he lends his talents as a copywriter and ghost writer to help clients from a range of industries find their brand and storytelling voices.

As a father and husband, his greatest joys are being a faithful loving husband to his wife LaKimbriea and father to his four children, Tiana (8), Catherine (18), Malik (21) and Jarell (23). As an author, he has ghost-written two books and is working on several projects including an autobiography examining his personal spiritual journey and a book outlining his experiences as a non-custodial parent. Rose credits his early upbringing in a military family growing up in Ansbach, Germany from age five to age 11 as one of his most endearing lifelong gifts.

While overseas, he encountered a plethora of cultures, people and experiences that shaped his world-view at a young age and allowed his consciousness to transcend the trivialities of race, religion, prejudice and negative societal constructs that infect the minds of men and plague humanity. He says his diverse childhood has perpetually enlightened his spiritual journey and ignited his soul with a humble flame of purpose. Ultimately, he understands he is an earthly vessel of the most high designed to fulfill a mission as *G.O.D.*, Generator, Operator and Director of a divine purpose.

Personal Profile

Key Words
1. Godly
2. Invictus
3. Triumphant
4. Perseverance
5. Committed

Favorite Quote
"I am G.O.D., the Generator, Operator & Director of my destiny!"

Values
Family, Leadership, Responsibility, Personal Transformation, Mutual Respect, Inner Vision, The Ability and Capacity to Dream, Succeed & Prosper

Marketable Skills
Copywriting & Editing, Digital Marketing Expertise, Public Speaking, Public Relations

Contact Information
Email: todsrose@gmail.com
Phone: (678) 634-1448
Website: todsrose.com
Search Services: budgetsearchpro.com
Writing Services: copycontentarticles.com

THE MALE PRINCIPLE AND THE SPIRITUAL ATTACK ON MANHOOD

Tod Rose

In any discussion of manhood today, a detailed examination of the male principle is paramount to a clear understanding. When you consider the malicious attacks men, particularly black men, face daily in our society, it is key to understand the depths of these attacks on manhood and their bearing on understanding the root of manhood; of which the male principle is key. To do this, I will have to visit antiquity and invoke what I like to call "God Science."

On our Men Magnifying Manhood Empowerment call recently, I was the guest speaker and I chose to focus my 10-15-minute presentation on the seven Hermetic principles, a.k.a. the axioms of Tehuti a.k.a. the Kemetic Laws of God depending on your spiritual system. As an avid fan and student of the bible, metaphysics, and all things spiritual, these principles changed the way I think and thus my life as it relates to my spiritual world view. The truth within these laws resonates in the fiber of creation itself and has led me to

174

understand that our reality is built on multiple plains, cosmic, spiritual and physical as the creator designed it. The principles are as follows:

- *Mentalism*
- *Correspondence*
- *Rhythm*
- *Cause and Effect*
- *Polarity*
- *Vibration*
- *Gender*

Each of these profound axioms is imbued with building blocks of the natural universe. On the levels where these laws were meant to coalesce and correspond we see a glimpse of the grand portrait of the Creator on all planes of existence according to spiritual law.

For the purposes of this discussion, we will focus on the principle of polarity, which we know in the physical plane as gender, i.e. male and female. The law of polarity states, *"Everything is Dual; everything has poles; everything has its pair of opposites; like and unlike are the same; opposites are identical in nature, but different in degree; extremes meet; all truths are but half-truths; all paradoxes may be reconciled."*

This powerful law of Polarity is also described in the language of the bible in the book of Genesis. The first instance comes in *Genesis 1:3-4: "God saw that the light was good, and he separated the light from the darkness."*

This passage represents the Creator's establishment of polarity as a building block of our universe with light and dark, representing the cosmic perspective. Going back to the spiritual laws, light and dark are the same only differing in degree. Here we also get a glimpse into the Creator's toolbox seeing how the spiritual laws facilitate one another in the process of creation. Later in Genesis, we get another distinct example.

Genesis 1:26 – "God created Man in his own image, in the image of God, he created him, male and female he created them."

Again, we see embedded in the creation of man and woman, the Creator's last act of creation, polarity which manifests on the physical plane as gender. For example, man and woman are both human beings and 99% physically identical, but emotionally and mentally just existing in slightly different degrees of vibration. Many would say that degree is equal to the distance between Mars and Venus, but I digress. Here we also see the biblical origins of divine order and authority in the example of the man coming forth first in the order of human creation. More to that point, we can all witness that it is in the male's nature to lead. Does the courtship ritual, both in the human and animal kingdom, begin with the males attempts to woo the female into being his mating? Need I ask who was the initiator of the courtship leading up to your current relationship or marriage? The characteristics of the male principle are clear in these three quick examples. More to that point, the male's role is to serve as the God head in the union of marriage and in the world.

In purely scientific terms, we all learned in basic science class that the most basic building blocks of all the physical universe is made of atoms. Each atom has both a positive and negative charge (+& -) which creates the force holding it together. The force that draws magnets together is a negative and positive charge attracting each other. This is in our hardwiring as humans on every level and a necessity for us to exist and continue to be fruitful and multiply as part of our biblical mandate. Our purpose as human beings is to create God's kingdom together, in unison, as man and wife and rule on earth like the God's we are. Jesus even said it in Psalms 82:6, *"I have said, ye are gods; all of you are children of the Most High."* We are creators endowed with creative powers physically, spiritually, and mentally (cosmically). As it were, the male carries the positive charge which he then delivers unto the negatively charged womb of his female counterpart thus wielding the peak of our divine powers of procreation. This process, when fulfilled under the divine institution and covenant of marriage, brings the creation of heaven on earth closer to reality.

As we have established, men and women as two sides of the divine creation equation. I also believe men and women have specific roles and inherent responsibilities dictated by their gender that also follow a divine order. When these natural gender principles and roles are thrown out of balance and twisted, the very foundation of creation is under attack. In real-time 2020 context, today, women marry women and raise children, men marry men and raise children, and the children are growing up confused about their own gender identities. Furthermore, with it getting harder and harder to distinguish women from men in appearance, it is quite easy to draw distinct parallels between the destruction of gender and the decline of the human condition.

Why Gender Roles Matter

Today, many people resent the term "gender roles" and I have always wondered why. After some thought and analysis, two things dawned on me. One, I realized the importance of gender roles are to a healthy balanced society. And two, I understand why the ruling evildoers are so persistent with perpetuating the anti-gender propaganda that has gripped popular media of late. Before I go too far, let me further define what I mean by gender roles and dispel the negative connotations of the word.

I recall my father telling me when I was young, "Son, you never let your lady mow the grass or take out the garbage." I took this type of thing to heart. He would also say a man takes care of his family and protects them. Occasionally, he would say these types of things to me in front of my mother and she would also chime in with a manhood quote of her own... "You're always supposed to treat your wife with respect and treat her well." Although I don't remember the exact places of times, growing up hearing those words stuck with me and seeing it being acted out by my parents, made it law in my mind and actions. In those things, I began to develop a concept of gender roles as a young man, but they shaped the behavior and temperament of respect towards the women in my life that I have today. I had learned the concept of gender roles and it set moral and behavioral boundaries once I began to explore relationships. On the other side of that token and from a male's perspective, I was also exposed to the concept of the female gender roles from things my mother would physically say and do with my sisters and the things I overheard her tell and teach my sisters; just like with my father but from a female perspective. Although I didn't realize it as a young boy, that knowledge completed the picture for me of the man-woman dynamic. I understood how the two work together on a level deeper than just the boys-have-different-parts-than-girls level. I had to tell this childhood anecdote to exemplify a point about how fulfillment of gender roles through the institution of marriage and raising of families creates the ideal environment to shepherd new souls, i.e. children into our physical realm.

1 Peter 3:7 - Likewise, ye husbands, dwell with [them] according to knowledge, giving honour unto the wife, as unto the weaker vessel, and as being heirs together of the grace of life; that your prayers be not hindered.

Under the authority of biblical principles, and within the loving fold of family, led by a principled man is the balance the world needs and simultaneously the target of the devil's attack. In a nutshell, the sanctity of our moral code as human beings is under evermore increasingly intense attack and men, who are by nature the protectors and the front lines of defense, are being decimated.

Defending Attack on Gender, Creation, and the Male Principle

We have established the cosmic, spiritual, and practical implications of the male principle and it should be clear to anyone with eyes today that the "trans" movement is just the latest phase of anti-gender and gender-blurring propaganda. The heaviest attack, in my opinion, has been levied on the male principle, the head, the first line of defense, of the family. Thus, the solution, the defense must be led by the true men among us and supported by the real women among us and carried on by the children we have reared together under Godly order and authority.

Psalm 127:3-5 – Behold, children are a heritage from the Lord, the fruit of the womb a reward. Like arrows in the hand of a warrior are the children of one's youth. Blessed is the man who fills his quiver with them! He shall not be put to shame when he speaks with his enemies in the gate.

This must start with the men.

Real Men, We Must Stand Up, Be Seen And Be Heard!

So, what does *standing up* look like? Men of God who realize their responsibility must begin to do three things more intently than ever. **First, men taking action individually, and collectively is what standing up looks like.**

1 Corinthians 16:13 - Watch ye, stand fast in the faith, quit you like men, be strong.

Men teach men how to be men. Manhood is a learned behavior. Even if an example of manhood in the form of a father, uncle or relative is not present directly for a young man to witness, he will seek this example. Too often, young men have the wrong examples to learn from which is why we must be that example. In the words of my favorite old-school rapper, "Each one, teach one." Individually, each man must commit to teaching one younger man how to be a man. Collectively, we should seek to join other men who represent manly ideals. Therefore, I joined and support Men Magnifying Manhood. We are a group of faithful godly men who accept, exemplify, and promote our responsibility as men and we are taking action! With the mission of magnifying manhood worldwide, we are collectively leading efforts to achieve an awakening of manhood in our society today through biblical principle. Visit menmagnifyingmanhood.com to learn more.

Secondly, as we act, we must strive to also be visible examples of manhood. From our individual faith to our collective actions, we are the biggest part of being a positive example is being visible. I'm reminded of a message delivered by Walt Harris (a fellow man who magnifies manhood) on our weekly empowerment call. As an ex NFL player, Walt drew a brilliant comparison between sports and real life saying that the impressions we receive in terms of our good deeds and works are like points on a scoreboard. Whoever receives the most impressions wins the game. He ended by saying that the enemy is getting more impressions that we are on the side of godliness. I am drawn back to this point from weeks ago because it is so profoundly true and relevant to my second point. In today's internet-ready world, where information and images are instantly available, the negative influences have dominated popular media.

180

Movies, television, music, games, and virtually every form of entertainment is permeated with negative influences. In this context, we must fight fire with fire in the sense that we must create and promote as many positive messages and images as possible to change the example that young men receive. We must replace drug dealing, and gang affiliation as the dominant images our young men receive. Can you imagine if those images were positive and promoting healthy relationships between men and women, and kingdom principles? We must individually and collectively create meaningful positive spectacles using the same media outlets that are perpetuating all the negativity. By creating, promoting, and transmitting images of what true manhood looks like and not allowing popular media to define what manhood looks and sounds like for society. We can recolonize the minds of our young men with impressions depicting examples of manhood from which behavior can be influenced. *It is paramount that we take back our image as men and redefine manhood in the eyes of young men and the world.*

Lastly, when we stand up, and become visible, we must also BE HEARD! So, what does *being heard* sound like? Pause for a moment and hear in your mind Dr. King's "I Have a Dream" speech during the march on Washington. I invoke this image and sound because at the time it was delivered, King was at the height of his conviction and purpose as a man of God. His voice attuned a nation to the vibration of God's authority that day and helped usher in a new age; likened to a modern-day Sermon on the Mount. When we, as men of God, speak with the conviction of our beliefs and faith, our voices resonate with that same energy and truth. This fact truly underscores the importance of us lifting our voices, speaking up and speaking out so that our truth can be heard. There is something about the power of the voice that pierces the veil and transmits truth like nothing else. Every major social change movement I can think of in the recent and distant past was pushed to its zenith by the vibration of voice transmitting a unifying message. Our sense of hearing is essentially our ears perceiving vibrations moving through air which in turn we receive both as audible sounds and as three-dimensional images in our mind's-eye. At its core, our ability to speak (create sound vibrations), hear (perceive sound vibrations) and interpret those sounds (create 3-D images of what those words represent in our mind) reveals yet another of our divine powers. The ancient universal law of vibration states that *"Nothing rests; Everything moves; Everything vibrates."* Taking this truth forward in our understanding, when a message is communicated through voices and it is received and understood through hearing, a common vibration is created beyond just hearing; the transmitter and receiver are "on the same vibe," so-to-speak. This commonality in understanding leads to a uniformity in action as we saw with the civil rights movement; further exemplifying the importance of voice and men speaking the truth about their commitment to shaping God's kingdom on earth.

Romans 10:17 - So faith comes from hearing, and hearing through the word of Christ.

When this occurs in mass as with Dr. King's groundbreaking speech, the world changes according to what has been spoken, in God's name. When true men of God speak truth, no ear can *unhear* it and it opens the way for reinstalling God as the head of all things and man as the righteousness head of the family once more. Men, it is up to us and the world is waiting for us to rise to our divine potential. It is time for us to stand up, be visible and be heard!

~Dedication~

Willie E. Rose (Grandfather, Valdosta, GA - Deceased)

Willie Mack Rose (Father, The Villages, FL)

James Edward Rose (Uncle, Conyers, GA - Deceased)

Alonzo Rose, Sr. (Great Uncle, Valdosta, GA – Deceased)

Jarell Jefferson-Rose (Son, Beaufort, SC)

Malik Sowell (Stepson, Atlanta, GA)

Deangelo Jamal Ellison Gray

Jaishawn Betts (Adopted Nephew)

Biography of Matthew Spriggs

Matthew Spriggs is from Prince George's County, Maryland, Holistic Health Educator, Media Personality, and former U.S. Army Reserve. He is the founder of Main Course Encouragement's Kingdom Health Talks and Co-Founder of Main Course Encouragement Media and Consulting. He operates as a multimedia production duo with his wife of over two years, Shanetta Spriggs, who specializes in social media marketing, design, interviews, content writing, and event coverage. Together, they are Main Course Encouragement providing exposure and engagement for entry, mid, and executive-level clients to connect while serving under-served communities to witness such events in order to inspire and activate change. Spriggs dedicates much time to learning and guiding the development of black health, faith, education, business, and services with most recent focus in STEM (Science Technology Engineering Mathematics) data science research and gammatic related events and projects.

Spriggs is the son of Sheila Spriggs and loving in-laws, Milton and Henrietta Monk. Loved by many family members, he is also a member of his originating church, Zion Hill Agape Baptist Church of Maryland. His home church is also pastored by his very own grandmother, Apostle June Taylor. In addition, he is a loved member of Word of Power World Church of Erwin, North Carolina, pastored by Mentor, Reverend Felton Smith.

You will find Spriggs active for mental, spiritual, and consumption wellness, autism awareness, technological advancement for both adults and children, highlighting black professionals and entrepreneurs, member of WOPWC Men Helping Men and most recent, Men Magnifying Manhood. Spriggs is dedicated to uplifting and advancing the Kingdom with all glory and reverence to the Father. His impact is beyond his own understanding, but with every venture, he is confident and upright in those plans.

Personal Profile

Key Words

Fortitude, Vessel, Hungry (Motivated)

Favorite Quote

"Too many of us are not living our dreams because we are living our fears." ~ Les Brown

Values

Faith, Family, Community, Healing, Encouragement

Marketable Skills

Multimedia Production, Holistic Health Process, Marriage, Public Speaking

Contact Information

Email+Google Hangouts: maincourseencouragement@gmail.com

Website: www.maincourseencouragement.com

Discussion Forum:
http://maincourseencouragement.com/discussion/

Instagram: www.instagram.com/maincourseencouragement

Linkedin: www.linkedin.com/in/shanetta-spriggs-5877ba98 (Shanetta Spriggs)

THE FIVE PILLARS OF MAN

Matthew Spriggs

T o truly begin to understand what a man is, what a man was, and what a man should be, I personally believe that it starts with YAH (God). The only way I would have known this is through my upbringing, and love that my family brought in my life; especially the women in my life. Growing up, I would say the women in my life had a very strong influence. They worked hard to provide; they were caring, nurturing, were strong and resourceful. I truly don't know how they did it. I realize it was something in them that kept that drive and determination going. I could write a million pages about just how thankful I am for them. Words can't explain as tears run down my face and a chill of elation run over my body. I love my family immensely. Now that you know my value of family, let's get a true understanding of what a man is more clearly. We must break down the word "man." My definition and understanding would be a generic term for Man or Womb-man, the two different versions of the male species. Those two different versions come in two forms of *fe*male and male. Deeper past the surface of what we believe is to receive a deeper and richer truth. With this newfound truth, you will obtain the ability to transform and magnify the man.

Growing up, I had a very strong female presence in my life and I wouldn't change it for anything in this entire world. I do understand now more clearly the significance of actually having a male figure in my life to show different things a man should do, how to react, process things from a different view, and think intentionally. Some of those things I did not get from the female perspective in my early years. I wouldn't say that I never had a male perspective either. I came from a family of hard workers, raised by my mother, grandma, aunts, and uncles. My mother and father separated when I was a toddler. I had six siblings; one of my brother's life was taken at an early age causing our lives to change forever. Being a big family in the city living under one roof was one thing, but to lose one of us so soon was another. I remember seeing a therapist along with my siblings to deal with the loss and having strong family members help us cope as well. The person with the biggest pain was my mother. To see her so lost and broken after the loss of her firstborn was crushing. My oldest brother was already a pillar for the family. He was smart, nimble, and reliable even at his young age. He had to grow up fast, but our village of family was there. He made me a triple peanut butter, jelly and sandwich one day for my birthday and it was the best gift I had ever received. When all three of those flavors along with the bread hit my taste buds, it was like a new light lit inside of me. See, I was known by my family as the "Garbage Disposal," so receiving something so inventive and edible was beyond what I could ever ask for at the time. Money was, of course, tight with so many people living in one house. We seldom ate something different, but John would always make a way to make playing in the house fun, to make a living on top of each other more bearable, and making food combinations that we could cherish for a lifetime. I dubbed him the coolest person ever. He was there in so many ways for my mother and for the rest of us and with the older members of the family helping out. It granted all of us to be able to still have a childhood despite growing up fast due to the surrounding circumstances.

I can confidently say it does take a village to raise a child. But as you can imagine, we all had that rife growing up because at the root of the foundation of the village starts with father, mother, and child. As I looked over my life thus far, I saw many things that could have molded me to become what the world believed a man was - to be "tough, to man up, not cry, stop acting like a girl," and the list goes on. I will say that I have been extremely blessed along the way to have different males perspectives come in my life to help me understand, and grow. Being a man really is an experience. You just can't be born a male and consider yourself a man. I say that because I have experienced it for myself and spoke with other men from different walks of life. I've spoken with many people who even had their father in their lives who still somehow ended up locked up, in trouble, mentally and emotionally unstable, and for a lack of better terms, not a full man. Now that's not to diminish or say that their fathers were poor leaders. But the result came from a sorry excuse of a male influence, which in my eyes, is worse than the absence of a father. At the end of the day, we can only take what people show us and then from there make a decision. That's one of the first things I learned about becoming and being a man. To take on relentless responsibility for whatever the outcome is and I believe that is what manhood is.

We put so much emphasis on what a man is and how a man should act with no substance or support behind it. Look around and see that there are those on a daily basis trying to check stuff off a list for their qualification of a man. I realized that a man is no different from a woman. I want to emphasize that because it highlights this egotistical, dominant being who is really weak because he has to compare himself to feel empowered, because the female version is named physically weaker by this society in this day and age. This is something I never understood because we were birthed by a woman, yet we have to have control or power over women and to me that made no sense at all. How can men disrespect where they come from? Where's the sensibility in knowing without them, there's no you, or any of us? Without man, there is no them. In actuality, most woman now could knock your block off. We must learn and grow in compassion to cherish, respect, and love each other and put down the defenses. Be present and respect the existence of one another. In this life, imparting love is the greatest act in the world.

Going back in time, I was directly impacted from facing the reality of the absence of core manhood in my mother's life. As kids, we did much walking to the metro, school and early jobs. I was an award-winning athlete for Suitland High School, worked at the harbor as a photographer and fast-food restaurants where I picked up some Spanish. Even though I was playing football, swimming, basketball, and breaking records along with my younger brother Marcus in baseball, there was still a stone in my mother's eyes. Even though my mother worked hard for all of us, she still carried the pain of losing Jon. It was still written all over her face.

I joined the United States Army directly after high school. I was able to travel and get out of that space temporarily. Though it was going well, I was falling into depression that I did not know was there. I was carrying her hurt and running from my own potential for true happiness. It was coming from what I was not fulfilling in my life as a whole man in tune with my spirit. This brings me to a structure I believe that will magnify manhood for generations to come: *The Five Pillars of Man.*

The First Pillar of what I believe magnifies manhood is something I learned from a woman. My grandmother instilled in us that the Father is the foundation of man as a whole. To trust in YAH, our Father God, to fear YAH (God), and to believe in YAH (God). YAH is the original name of our Lord in Hebrew. This alone is the key to it all. To also support that, when I was little, my oldest cousin, now Reverend Brandon or "Mr. B" as we would call him, gave me a bible and highlighted a Scripture inside of it for me. And to this day, it is still my favorite Scripture. That Scripture is Proverbs 3:5-6: *"I will trust in the Lord with all thy heart and lean not unto thy own understandings. In all thy ways I will acknowledge him and he shall direct thy path."* Without YAH (God), there is no me. There's no existence, and there is no life. To come into that truth is what truly separates and distinguishes a real man.

The Second Pillar I learned was from a man; the many men I mentioned earlier who added to my understanding. I was taught to respect, love, cherish, protect, comfort, and learn the woman because every man on this earth came from a woman. So it will be almost foolish...No, it is foolish to disrespect, condemn, abuse, and misuse them in any kind of way, whether physically, mentally, sexually, and emotionally. I learned at a very young age that women are simply phenomenal, tremendous beings of YAH (God). He had to put us to sleep to form and create this woman and if that doesn't tell you something, then you are still asleep. We should recognize this great woman she was intended to be in His eyes. Such a miracle! As I read Yahweh's (God's) Word, you could only fathom such miracles. When you treat them right, you will witness seas parting. It reminds me of when Yeshua (Jesus) fed the multitude. Now just imagine the woman supplementing that full course meal. The Word never lies. Yeshua (Jesus) spoke over our pending ability to do even greater things than this and I am for one a firm believer and witness. My grandma would make a pot of beans and drop biscuits that appeared never-ending to feed all of us. I want to remind you to never forget the womb-man. I do mean all women; to cherish, support, protect, be honest with, and offer compassion for their expertise in those areas and beyond. With their love, understanding, and flexibility, you will never be disappointed. I learned that as a man we must be emotionally stable and mentally capable to be that support and stronghold as men who will always be meant to be to one of YAH's (God's) greatest creations.

 The Third Pillar is self. To truly understand oneself, you must be born again. That's to die to this old, dead, and played out belief that people, society, and life gave us. We must seek the truth and use common sense. To unlock yourself is another great gift we could never open. This as you might have already guessed, unlocks the door to your potential. In order to develop into a REAL man, you have to know the basics on how to take care of yourself. With age, I learned how to clean - I mean deep clean, cook, wash my own clothes and body, how to fix things, how to shop for food, hold a door, and be a gentleman. To me, this is just basic etiquettes to life in general that everyone should know. I have learned that no one can push you to the next level. You must obtain the desire for that elevation for yourself. Unfortunately, that leaves a huge problem if you allow it, because there is only one thing that can stop you and that's YOU. So don't ever sell yourself short. Refrain from making excuses about your past, about how you were raised or your life circumstances. Though those things provide a vital story, it's a story you can rewrite and not sulk in. Don't claim the life given to you; claim the result of your life from fortitude through those obstacles. Access a higher level by demanding a better you in how you grow, develop, and use your mind. Implement this daily.

Each choice you make will produce a result, no matter how big or small. In order to make this shift, you must focus and remove what doesn't align with your newfound perspective, the real, authentic version of your-SELF. Remember, *you* are responsible for you.

The Fourth Pillar is the molding process; the trial and error, in which we go through pain, hardship, disappointments, and magnification. This molding process is yours and it is unique, so value it. It tests and convicts your very being. It holds you accountable to the very essence of who you are. The challenges of life will come to test you in ways that are big and some small. The importance of this modular development reminds me of being trusted with little, so I could be trusted with much. Whether you steal a piece of candy from the store or rob a bank, you are still a thief. It's that kind of responsibility and challenge as men we must face and conquer. These trials and temptations come in various forms and seem personalized just for you. They can be in the form of woman, money, drugs, food, _____ and more to be named. *(Place your vice in that blank space).*

It can be one or many, but the great thing is that I want you knowledgeable of your victory. Remain in the will and mold of the Father. You have the strength to overcome because no temptation will be placed on you that you can't bear. You can make it through any and every variation of trials, mistakes, and downfalls. As a man, we have to be in control. Allow my clarity to remind you that we are never in control of people. What we can control is our very own emotions and actions. As the head of the family unit, that doesn't mean dictatorship; that means you just received more responsibility, accountability, and pressure. If you step up to that threshold of true manhood, then no woman, person, thing, or non-man, can challenge you. I know we heard that with great power comes great responsibility and that is the simple truth. How we use all that we have learned and experienced, measures what is going to dictate the outcomes of our lives.

The Fifth Pillar is action; taking all we learned from and throughout the first Four Pillars and implementing them throughout your everyday life. We as men have lost our perspective through unqualified people who we allowed to govern our lives. It's as if we lost our integrity of true manhood. We are in a system were the woman is the foundation, and in the right context yes; but it's misguided because they were forced into that role. We the men stop being that foundation, to support, to build, to grow, to protect, to encourage, and most importantly, to love because of an assumption of what a man is in today's world. That impacts the next boy and girl directly. We have pretty much been summed up with interest in only; work, eat, sex, sports/entertainment, and sleep. We stop taking action and having substance. I want to leave you with a sense of purpose, duty, empowerment, and refinement, as a man. Take back your position in the spirit.

I was told that you are only as strong as the weakest person on your team. I make it a mission to empower anyone I am around. There's no greater joy for me than to do that. I know that the Father has blessed me to be a vessel for His use and I want my family members to have a seat at the table. I want them to tell me what they have learned, where they have gone, and who they have become. There is room for all of us. I'm proud to say that my mother is no longer in that lost and sad place. I'm no longer depressed. I'm married to my beautiful devoted wife who inspired more pillars of purpose. Everything I am even back to my brother Jon, impacts what I consume daily. I've met great people and I had to get there by way of these Five Pillars. We have to empower each other as one body. You are not just a male. Let's redefine what a man and manhood is.

Join me in driving that forward action onward. Become these Five Pillars. Go out and fight the good fight, and keep the faith. I am a YAH (God) fearing, believing, woman loving, self-knowing, overcoming, and action-taking man, magnifying manhood.

~Dedication~

YAH (God)

Shanetta Spriggs (my wife)

Sheila Spriggs

June Taylor

Jon Spriggs

Marcus Spriggs

Marie Spriggs

Martin Hughes

Jonathan Spriggs

Ricardo Spriggs

Sharon Spriggs

Mary Blanchard

James Spriggs, Jr.

Maurice Spriggs, Sr.

Daniel Shaw

Maurice Spriggs, Jr.

Brandon Spriggs

The Entire Spriggs Family & Village

The Pearson-Monk Family

Biography of Dr. Perry E. Tankard, Sr.

Dr. Perry E. Tankard, Sr. is a Pastor (Bishop-Elect), Evangelist, Soul Winner, Teacher, Author, Business Man, Father, Mentor, Husband, friend and encourager to many. He is the Founder of Power In The Word Ministry & Evangelistic Association, Impact Community Development Corporation, the "School of Evangelism" and various business entities.

He co-founded with his wife a house cleaning business earning $20 to $50,000 annually, a church from $62.50 to $750,000 annually in five years and a health care business from $350 to $470,000 per year with 30 employees.

Dr. Tankard believes that "through faith, nothing can be impossible" by using the principles of the Word of God. He instilled in his children the following wise counsel: (1) Get a good education, (2) Seek a quality career, and (3) Look for creative ways to make money with a business of your own. His mother always taught him, "Take Jesus to keep you!"

He is active in setting up 501 (c) (3) non-profit organization for churches and community groups as well as church charters, by-laws, etc. He consults with Christian businesses and churches for growth/development of their congregations. He sits on the board of three church/ministry organizations and three non-profit organizations. He has been in ministry since 1984 conducting

197

miracle revivals, crusades, workshops and seminars. He is co-author of two books and a television/radio personality.

Dr. Tankard and his wife are the parents of nine children and 13 grandchildren; he has an older married daughter with five children. They have raised them in the fear and admonition of the Lord. They have this testimony that "God will always make a way. It's not over until we win!"

Personal Profile

Key Words

Courageous, Industrious, Courteous, Innovative, Beyond

Favorite Quote

"Do something even if it's wrong. Get up and make something happen."

Values

Enterprising, Industrial, Networker, Visionary, Encourager to others

Marketable Skills

Public Speaking, Organizing, Consultant Leading, Networking, Financial Source

Contact Information

Email: powerintheword1800@yahoo.com

Website: https://getallexicited.wixsite.com/website

LinkedIn.com: Perry Tankard

Phone/Text: (919) 949-1970

RAISING GODLY SONS TO BE MEN IN AN UNGODLY SOCIETY

Dr. Perry E. Tankard, Sr.

In our society, there are many obstacles for black men to endure. And excuses that we give for our shortcomings. We have to come to grips that God, families, the Body of Christ and society will not accept these for our continued failure and negative behavior. I will be transparent with some events of my own life, things that have shaped me into who I am today; a man, father, husband, man of God, friend and mentor to preachers.

My prayer is that the readers can look in the mirror into the depths of their soul, draw from the Holy Spirit and find strength to be reshaped and remolded by God. To become all that we can be for His glory and honor. While none of us are perfect, we strive for perfection in God daily. The testimonials from this work should find us all as we relate it to our own lives.

199

Part of the problem is for decades, slavery had a negative effect on the black culture. The tearing away of the father and displacement of the children have taken a toll on black families. Through the Willie Lynch Syndrome that was instituted to separate slaves, we must be set free in our spirits from the slave mentality. We must forgive the harshness that our ancestors endured. Toughness and tenacity within should cause us to arise and be the best you that you can be.

We must look to the future, as we are the future. Our seed has a legacy to emulate. Black males should not lack in guidance that can catapult their destiny and allow them to leave a legacy of their own.

THE PROBLEM

We have bought into Satan's lie that we can never be anything, came from nothing and can never do anything positive. That is a lie from the pits of hell. If we recognize and defy that mindset, we can accomplish great things. "Looking unto Jesus who is the Author and finisher of our faith…" (Hebrews 12:2a). Take the Psalmist David's example: Encourage yourself in the Lord. Draw from that inner strength as a man of God and not let the devil defeat you.

We have been overlooked in the workplace, community, family and the church. We have to get over it and move to the next level. We can be defeated by the devil or defeat the devil with the Word of God. We cannot allow our emotions, criticism, unfairness and the like to hinder us.

<u>MY STORY</u>

I was born in Wardtown, Virginia, a town of less than 400 currently. As a boy, my focus was on school, church and vegetables that we had to harvest for a living. I attended Ebenezer Baptist Church with my mother, Mae E. Parker and my three older siblings. All of us had different fathers, but we were a close-knit bunch.

My mother married Robert Parker (her second marriage) and my baby sister Glenda was born. Her first marriage was to John Tankard, whose brother was Arthur, the Father of Ben Tankard, The Godfather of Gospel Jazz, a Pastor and television star of "Thicker than Water." Cousin Ben is what I call him.

"Everybody is from somewhere." That was my humble beginnings and you never forget where you came from. I remember going to the daycare, back then called the Nursery. My teacher taught me my ABC's and 123's, preparing me for the first and second grades in Virginia.

In the second grade, we performed a play about George Washington and Abraham Lincoln. I volunteered to be both since no one wanted the part of Abraham Lincoln. How would we pull this off you may ask? Well, my teacher said that I could switch costumes in the middle of the play. George had a white wig and Abe had a black stovepipe hat. While the other children had 5-10 lines, I had 62 lines to learn and recite. I went home and my big sister Joyce confidently said, "You will learn each one of these lines. I was able to recite all my lines without missing one and changed costumes in a timely manner to make the play a big hit.

I attribute this incident in giving me the confidence to learn the Word of God as a preacher. I teach others to learn the Word of God from memory and have the confidence that it can be done. Maybe my teachers knew that I would be a preacher of the Gospel way back then.

I remember walking to the strawberry field before school. However, as any seven-year-old, I ate more than I picked. In the summer, we picked potatoes, tomatoes, cabbages, and cucumbers. This is how we made a living and how we ate, carrying home some of the crop at the end of the day.

My grandmother, Mrs. Annie Bull Kellum, did domestic work for the neighbors, just like the movie, *The Help*. She preserved the fruits and canned the vegetables so we could eat in the winter. She made quilts from her sewing scrap materials, which kept us warm in the winter. We lived with her when our mother was preparing to move the family to Sussex County, Delaware. She was an extraordinary woman and the mother of eight children, while three of them died as children from various things. Those who survived were ever Aunt Lillian, Uncle James, my mother, Uncle Sonny, and Uncle Clyde Bull. My dear grandmother would have gifts for everyone on Christmas and had them waiting for us. She and her children were instrumental in shaping my life and perception of life and success while I grew up. I saw my uncles as strong family men who took care of their families.

After the passing of her husband and my grandfather, Henry Bull, she remarried William (Bill) Kellum, an extraordinary man. He never had any children, but adopted all of us as his own. The farmers hired him to harvest the vegetables and gather people to work. He could neither read nor write, but man, could he count some money! He took a stick and wrote in the sand the number of sacks of vegetables or bushel baskets of potatoes picked so he could pay the workers on Fridays. By watching him, I believe I gained my counting money skills from him which came in handy as I grew into adulthood.

William helped our family tremendously and always kept me close by his side. When he drove the farmer's tractor, I was in the seat steering the wheel. When he drove the truck down the middle of the potato field, I sat in the driver's seat, holding it in the row, going down the field. I was only four years old and I tell people that I honestly have been driving since age four or five.

My mother, now the retired Pastor Mae Parker cared for her five children, but I remember her helping a single father care for his little daughters. His wife had passed and she reached out to them periodically. It is one thing to say that you are a Christian; it is another to show love and act it out. We did not know the Word of God the way we do now, but she was acting on God's Word the best way she knew how.

Our church, the Ebenezer Baptist Church in Wardtown, was a traditional Baptist church and a pillar in the community. I remember going to Sunday school and sitting by the oil heater for the Sunday school lesson. This was the first church that I can remember attending. Vividly, I remember the choir in their robes and caps with tassels, singing the songs of Zion.

WHO IS YOUR DADDY?

I do not know much about my biological father, but I do know that his name was Stanly Emerson Chisum, born on the Eastern Shore of Virginia. I knew his first cousin, Justine Harman who had been raised with him. She always treated me good and was his favorite cousin. After I was born, he moved to Delaware and started a family. I never remember seeing him until later years when we moved to the State of Delaware in the summer of 1966.

THE DELAWARE YEARS - MY DAD

My mom and step-dad went to a town called Berlin, Maryland to find work and a place to live. My brother graduated from high school in 1965 and attended Norfolk State University. My sister Joyce, who graduated in 1966, lived with our grandma, earned her diploma, and then enrolled at Norfolk State University as well.

We settled in Roxana, Delaware, a suburb of Selbyville; current population 2,167. You could say that I was reared in "small town America." I take great pride in knowing that anyone can achieve anything no matter what family he or she are born in or what town they grew up in. God is no respecter of persons; He will use whomever He chooses, wherever He wants. HE is GOD!

Where my Stepfather worked, a man and his wife built a new home and rented their old house to us. His wife worked at the local poultry plant and got my mom a job. This house was on a main street in the community. After school and during the summer, I would be out in the yard playing. A man rode by daily and kept looking my way. He was afraid to stop, but I could tell that he wanted to. One day he stopped and called my name out. I looked up to answer and he introduced himself. He asked if I know who he was and then told me that he was my dad. He lived down the street with his wife and two daughters. I learned later that my mother did not want him to be around me. Thirty years later, I had the privilege to lead him to Jesus Christ, was his pastor for two years and baptized him and my younger sister and brother.

The only consistent man in my life was my stepfather. After work, he threw pitches to me as I pretended to be the catcher. He was a strong lefty and they always stung, but I did not let him know. In the African-American community, Christian and non-Christian alike, we seem to have a stigma of absentee fathers and the role of stepfathers. From a DNA or biological standpoint, it has confused many children. You are carrying one man's DNA and reared by another man's ideology. Many things that we become are because of things that are programmed in our lives because of our biological fathers. Others are because of being products of our environment.

Over a period of time, I watched my stepfather become distant from the family. He claimed that he was hanging out with the guys at the bar. It was discovered that he was having an affair with a younger woman. What a crazy mixed up world we live in! Sin, the bible says, when it is finished, it brings forth death. I witnessed the death of the only family I knew. I use to think that my cousins had it made. They had both biological parents in the home, my Uncles James, Milton and Clyde.

After meeting my dad, he would always put a $20 bill in my hand when he saw me. That was his way of saying, "I love you." We all show love in different ways. After all, I was still his oldest child. He told me later that whenever he decided that he wanted to marry someone, he always told them that he had a son. That would prove valuable advice for me later in life.

One thing the Word of God teaches us in Proverbs 6:20 and Proverbs 1:8, is not to forsake the law of your father and mother. It did not stipulate if they were saved or unsaved. My dad taught me some valuable life lessons; I took them to heart and implemented them into my life.

We need to realize that we cannot determine how we got here; if it was from a loving family unit, a relationship that came from fornication, adultery or even rape. We should be thankful to God for our existence and be the best you that you can be. We did not get to choose who our parents were. We could have been aborted or miscarried. Do you know that if you were born after 1973, you could have been legally aborted and never thought of again?

All my mother's children were their fathers' first born and each of us had to take care of them in their last years. The love of Jesus Christ supersedes anything that was done and I am so thankful that it does. Jesus Christ coved our sins with His blood and I am so thankful that He did. Anything, no matter how bad it seems, has been washed in His blood and cast into the Sea of Forgetfulness.

MY SCHOOL YEARS

Upon settling in Roxana, Delaware, my third grade year began around 1965. It was at the end of segregation and the beginning of integration of school systems across the country. In Virginia, we went to all black schools and now we were able to attend white schools. First, I was enrolled at the local black elementary school and began making new friends. My cousin Tony moved with his family from Virginia and we were classmates.

Because the school district said that we lived in another area, I was transferred to Roxana Elementary School. It was a small three-room schoolhouse and had one teacher for Grades 1-2, 3-4, and 5-6. For the first time, I attended class with white boys and girls.

The school was so small that the principal would have to pick up some of the students in his little Studebaker, me included. He taught us how to make kites from newspaper. These kites would actually fly in the strong Delaware breeze. I went to my teacher the last day of school and thanked her for being my teacher. She thanked me with a startled look on her face as if no other student had ever said that to her; especially not a little third grade black boy.

After that year, the school closed and all the students were bussed to the middle school. Mr. Johnson, the principal, had been a friend and he loved all the kids in that three-room schoolhouse. That school lived on in my heart and in 1993, almost 30 years later, as a pastor in Burlington, N.C., we started Mt. Zion Christian Academy. It was the first predominately African-American Administered School in Alamance County, North Carolina. It was housed in three classrooms with three teachers teaching multiple grades. It brought back memories of the little Red School House in Delaware. Occasionally, I would tell our students the story with tears in my eyes. God knew what He was doing sending me to that school.

Men, be encouraged and know that the path you were put on helped to shape us into what God would have us to become. If we look back, we can see the hand of God. We all made mistakes that we may be ashamed of today. Things that may have brought us pleasure or those others influenced us to do. To God be the Glory for how He brought us to where we are today.

Many of us would not be the men of God that we are today if our biological fathers, spiritual fathers, and other positive male role models had not taken interest in us. If the men in my community had not looked out for me, would I have been able to keep a job, raise a family and successfully take care of them, and educate them, etc.?

My first salvation experience was one that I will remember and cherish for the rest of my life. It was at St. Matthews Baptist Church in Bishopville, Maryland on the Mason-Dixon Line that separates the north from the south. My mother came home from work and said to me, "We having a revival this week and this could be your week!" Therefore, I prepared myself to go that night. The visiting woman evangelist preached and the altar was filled. I remember being at the altar with some of my school mates, as one of the Church mothers stood at the altar. The old saints had us to "Call Jesus!" I tried to get up several times, but she urged me to "stay there until Jesus came in." Come in He did as I felt the power of God flood my soul! I felt the peace and joy that is unspeakable and full of glory. Although I had given my life to Jesus, I did not fully understand all that had transpired. Unlike today's churches with follow-up teams, I knew that I had experienced salvation, but could not explain it from the Word of God. From there, I became a Junior Trustee of the church.

Throughout my junior high years, I was an "A" and "B" student, played basketball, and sang in the school choir. I remember having a solo in the musical, *Jesus Christ, Superstar*. In the ninth grade, I lost interest in my schoolwork. I still was on the basketball and track and field teams from 10th - 12th grades. However, other things began to take over my interest. I would work after school, and be too tired to do my schoolwork. By my senior year, I was indulging in things that usually grab the attention of young people.

FAST FORWARD

After graduating in 1975, I chose to attend Durham Business College on an invitation to play basketball by my brother-in-law, Coach Reginald Terry. There he inspired me to major in business because, "the world is business." In my freshman year, my girlfriend, who was back home became pregnant. Coach Terry suggested I get a job ASAP. He gave me his car and told me to go to Hardee's fast-food restaurant and they hired me. My daughter, Kim was born in September of 1976.

I was able to obtain a two-year degree and then a Bachelor of Science Degree from St Augustine's University in Raleigh. Upon completing the first two legs of my education, I returned to Durham to work in the fast food industry. After rededicating my life to the Lord in April of 1980, I prayed that God would send me a wife. I made a vow to him that when He did, I would be faithful to her and the children He would bless us to love and care for.

In October of 1980, I met my future bride (the former Rona Reeves). After going to church services and dinner dates, I knew this was the woman God had sent me. Taking my father's advice, I told her that I had a daughter who was four years old at the time. We were married June 20, 1981 and started out on a now 38 years together in raising our nine children, starting, building business ventures, and over 35 years of ministry. Through many trials, shortcomings, and hardships, we are still standing.

MY FIVE SONS

I have had the honor of raising five young men and four young women in the fear and admonition of the Lord. They have only known me as a Christian, man of God and a preacher all their lives.

I started out with the purpose of raising my sons to be godly men and have strived to be an example to them and advise them to turn to Jesus and His Word for everything.

I am thankful for the examples I had growing up with men from my community and church. I am thankful for my college professors, ministers, bishops, businesses owners, etc. I urge my boys, now men, to seek wise council from good men. I make myself available to hear from and communicate with them on business matters and family matters. I purposed to set a godly example and show them how I had to maneuver things around to make things work. They would be men, husbands and fathers one day. Four are grown and three are married with children.

Whenever there was a family situation, I would take the oldest boys with me. We had the big snow of 1999 and had to walk to the store to get food. Therefore, my oldest two son went with me. Some of the things that I taught them while growing up were:

1. Pray about everything because God knows all and has an answer in His Word. Keep a relationship with Him and He will keep a relationship with you.

2. Live holy and repent often for we know that Jesus could come at any time when you think not. Always live your life as if He was coming back within the next hour.

3. Work hard at everything you put your hands to. God said that He would bless the works of your hands (Deuteronomy 28:8). He can only bless what you put your hands to do.

4. Always put your best foot forward. If folks see you trying, they may lend you a hand. God and people help those who help themselves.

5. Do not mess around with a woman that you do not intend to marry. Child support could be $200 a week or more. Pay it or see the inside of a jail. And guess what? It will still be there when you get out. Some other man may raise your child and then there is not much you can say.

6. Fast, pray, and seek God early. We usually make a mess when we try to work things out on our own. We end up coming back to him anyway.

I have seen them evolve into the men they are today; married, raising their families in the fear and admonition of the Lord; working hard and striving to provide for their families. I used to wonder how our kids would turn out. I see that we as men have a very important role to play in the lives of the children we father and bring into this world.

In summary, I am so grateful for the godly impact I feel I had on my boys, now men as they came through the stages of life. I can see the positive effects that I made in them by being there every step of the way. I made a commitment to God that if He sent me a wife that I would stick it out no matter what. I have kept my word and God has surely kept His! Great is His faithfulness!

~Dedication~

Andrew Bull, Alexandria, VA (Big Brother)
Reginald Terry, Birdsnest, VA (Brother-In-Law)
William Covington, Durham, NC (Brother-In-Law, Posthumous)
Robert Parker, Berlin, MD (Stepfather, Posthumous)
Pastor James Bull, Baltimore, MD (Uncle)
Evangelist Milton Bull, Exmore, VA (Uncle)
Perry E. Tankard II, Durham, NC (Oldest Son)
Jeremy Tankard, Garner, NC (Son)
Victor Tankard, Raleigh, NC (Son)
Daniel Tankard, Durham, NC (Son)
Joshua Tankard, Durham, NC (Son)
Fabien McCray, Sr., Dagsboro, DE (Son-In-Law)
Fabien McCray, Jr., Dagsboro, DE (Grandson)
Jaylen Griffin, Dagsboro, DE (Grandson, Posthumous)
Jack Beckett, Millsboro, DE (High School Basketball Coach)
Pastor Gene Rentrope, Durham, NC (Family Friend)
Willie Neal, Durham, NC (College Friend)
Bishop Gary Wayne Cooper, Wadesboro, NC
(College Roommate)
Pastor John McKnight, Durham, NC (Friend)
Pastor Irvin Taborn, Durham, NC (Friend)
William (Bill) Kellum, Wardtown, VA
(Step-Grandpa, Posthumous)
Men of my church/community, Sussex County Delaware
Perry III, Timothy, Roman, Philemon, Nehemiah, Zephaniah,
Courtney, Jeremiah, Grayson of NC (Grandsons)
Alvin Lee Chisum, Eastern Shore of MD, (Little Brother)

STANLEY E. CHISUM , VA, DE, GA, FL
(My Dad, Posthumous)

Biography of Rev. Dr. Mark Thompson

Born: Akron, Ohio

Married: 42 Years,
                    Stephanie Thompson

Family: Two Children, Five Grandchildren (ages five - 22 years old)

Father in Ministry: Dr. George Moore

Pastoral History: New Bethel AME, Lithonia, Georgia, Big Bethel AME, Atlanta, Georgia, Allen Temple AME, Cincinnati, Ohio Redemptive Life Christian Fellowship, Snellville, Georgia

Education: Akron University, B.A., The Interdenominational Theological Center (ITC), Masters of Divinity, United Theological Seminary, Doctorate of Ministry

Adjunct Professor: Beulah Bible College, McAfee School of Theology, The Interdenominational Theological Center

Years in Ministry: 30 Years

Years Pastoring: 25 Years
Ministry Mission: Teach the Word, Touch the Soul, Transform the Life

Personal Profile

Key Words
Teaching the Word, Touching the Heart, Transforming the Life

Favorite Quote
Don't just go through it, grow through it.

Values
Spiritual and Ethical Integrity, Building Lives, Providing the necessary tools for individuals to claim their God-given Gifts and Purposes

Marketable Skills
Preaching, Teaching, Administration, Innovation

Contact Information
Email: pastort333@mac.com

Website: www.theredemptivelife.org

Church Contact: 770-922-1234

MEN BEING MEN

Rev. Dr. Mark W. Williams

B eing a man means many things to many people. Depending on where you were born; depending upon your cultural surroundings; depending upon those whom you may have idolized, your definition of what a man is, is as diverse as there are days in the year. Community, culture, historical tendencies and family are arguably the greatest influences that shape a child into what a man will become. What is seen in the home, what expressions are exhibited by one's parental authority, what is witnessed from patriarchs and matriarchs or extended family all become the building grounds by which young boys develop their cues on what a man should be. The problem though is that what is seen, observed, or what has become the norm does not necessarily adhere or align itself with biblical principles nor with ethical or moral norms. So then, the purpose of this article is to shed light on a particular cultural trend that is not only practiced in unenlightenment by men, but likewise, toxic to women as well as family structures. Specifically, what does it mean for a woman to be submissive, and, what does Scripture means when it says that a husband is the head of his wife?

As a former student of mine and now friend stated correctly, "The role of women in church leadership is primarily understood through a lens of three New Testament books: 1 Corinthians, Ephesians, and 1 Timothy."[1] I would add that leadership roles were not only addressed by Paul, but relationship roles, or what's known as the "Household Codes" were also a part of Pauline literature. Of the three passages referenced, I will share two of the more misquoted or better stated, misunderstood passages in the Epistles. In Ephesians 5:22 (NRSV), Paul writes: "Wives, be subject/submissive to your husbands as you are to the Lord." In 1 Corinthians 11:3 (NRSV), Paul writes: "But I want you to understand that Christ is the head of every man, and the husband is the head of his wife, and God is the head of Christ."

It is in the two terms "subject or submissive" and "head" where the roles of women, but more so the misunderstood roles of men have caused so much division in the community, the home, and in particular, in the minds of men. To say it another way, men as well as women have used those two Scriptures and the two particular terms as their authority on how women should be treated. When women do not respond to the dictates of those two terms (submissive or head), men have viewed their lack of adherence as a sign of disrespect regarding their authority.

As a pastor who has counseled through pastoral care sessions, many have been the times when couples have come for marital intervention, where the man states "she does not follow or respect

---

[1] Hamilton, Thomas. Beulah Heights University, 2008

me as the head of the household." Whereby, the woman will respond by saying "I have rights, I have a mind, and why should I follow someone who is wrong?" Though I have oversimplified the scenario, the heart of the issue goes much deeper.

From a historical perspective, men and women have been raised with the understanding that indeed the husband is the "head of the house." That means, what the man says, goes. The understanding comes from, I would argue, not only cultural practices and traditions, but also from the writing of the Apostle Paul. Even in my own home as a child, I witnessed day after day how my father would come home from work, and my mother, who as a housewife, would literally serve him, placing his food on the table in front of him, and seemingly follow every instruction that he gave; this was part of her familial norm and cultural understanding. Many times as I witnessed their relationship, my mother would literally be devalued as an individual because her only place in the familial hierarchy was to serve her husband who was the head of the house. Though my father was never mean spirited in demeanor, nor was my mother fearful or disrespected by any means, and though it was absolutely clear that they loved each other, the roles in the marriage were clearly defined; he was the head of the house and she would follow. I further share that there were many times where I witnessed my mother's countenance as one that was almost servant like in appearance, even to the point of occasional tears. I have no doubt that because we were a faithful church going family, that my father and mother were strict adherents to Scripture, faithful to the words of Paul, all coupled with a strong dose of cultural tradition. The problem though is that Paul's writings, as stated above, have been misquoted and/or misunderstood.

To understand what Paul was talking about I would share a brief theological study on the Scriptures' reference as a means of bringing clarity to what Paul wrote. I do this for one purpose, to increase men's, husbands', and fathers' understanding that no man has to lord over or rule any woman to fully be a man. I'll say it in another way. Anyone, whether man or woman who believes that they have the God-given right to regulate someone else's life in order to have order in the home or to gain some inner-sense of self-confidence, not only operates with internal dysfunction, but their mindset points to a total lack of understanding as to what Scripture is really saying.

First, when men read the word "subject" or "submissive" in the King James vernacular, as in "wives be submissive to your husbands," they too often promote verse twenty-two at the expense of verse twenty-one which reads: "Be subject to one another out of reverence for Christ." The word "subject" (*hypotasso*) is a Greek verb which means to voluntarily submit one's authority to another. If you study the definition, Paul is saying that both husbands and wives have authority in the marital relationship, but there are times when each of them must voluntarily relinquish their authority for the good of the relationship or for a decision that must be made. So then, not only are women to be submissive to husbands, but husbands according to verse twenty-one are to be submissive to wives. The reason is very simple; man doesn't have all the answers; neither do women have all the answers. When God put a man and a woman together, they—prayerfully—were equally yoked and come together to abide in unity. So the first instruction on men being men is understanding that a man's role is to relinquish the role, and I dare say, the expectation of having anyone under their control; God made our spouses to be by our side and not under our foot. Walking together always supersedes and brings greater holistic value to a relationship, but particularly, to the individual. Further, dominance, control or power can never increase a man's credibility, but equality, partnership, and working as a unit does. Our worth is affirmed and increased by helping—where we are able—others to become the person God created them to be, and that truth goes both ways. Paul's teaching to the Church of Ephesus was centered on unity in the family of Christ, not in authority over one's spouse.

Having said this, we look at Paul's letter to the Church of Corinth where he writes: "...the husband is the head of his wife." The English definition of the word "head" has many definitions, but the one most understood based upon the context of Paul's writing means one who is in charge of something or someone. So when the word "head" is understood from a western perspective, it means that the man is in charge of the woman, he is the lead, and she is to follow. However, the word "head" in the Greek translation has variable definitions as does the English version. Head is the word (*Kephale*) in the Greek language. According to Richard A. Horsley, "The standard reading of 'head' in the metaphorical sense of authority is rarely attested to in Greek."[2] In fact, the Greek meaning for "head" has multiple figurative meanings, but none of them include authority, a superior, or someone who has higher rank than another. The Greek word "*rosh*" was "the more common term used for a ruler, commander, leader or chief."[3] So then, the first thing we must understand as it relates to the roles of a man in relationship with a woman, is that Paul's writing has a different meaning for "head" than what the English language bears.

Again, the Scripture: "But I want you to understand that Christ is the head of every man, and the husband is the head of his wife, and God is the head of Christ," is challenging from a Trinitarian perspective. John's Gospel records in Chapter one, "In the

---

[2] Horsley, Richard A. 1 Corinthians, Abingdon New Testament Commentaries (Nashville: Abingdon Press, 1998), p. 153.

[3] Ibid.

beginning was the Word and the Word was with God, and the Word was God. He was in the beginning with God. All things came into being through him, and without him not one thing came into being. What has come into being in him was life, and the life was the light of all people." Then we go down to verse 14, which says: "And the Word became flesh and lived among us, and we have seen his glory, the glory as of a father's only son, full of grace and truth (John 1:1-4, 14, NRSV). While Paul's writing suggests (by visual examination) that God came first and then came Jesus, an exegetical treatment of John's Gospel shares two components of the Trinitarian unity of God the Father, and God the Son. The two passages of Scripture—John's and Paul's—appear to be in opposition to each other, but in fact are saying one and the same thing.

In Jesus—from a Trinitarian perspective—we witness the wisdom, the redemption and the love of God in the flesh of the Son. Therefore, when Paul writes that God is the "head" (*Kephale*) of Jesus, the proper translation and meaning is the word "source." So then, Paul's writing and John's are not in opposition when the translation of the scripture is properly fitted to read as follows: "But I want you to understand that Christ is the (source) of every man, and the husband is the (source) of his wife, and God is the (source) of Christ." So then, the word "source" is one of the variable meanings of the word "head" or the Greek word *Kephale*, but there's a reason why Paul stated it in this way.

In the book of Genesis, there are at minimum two accounts of God's creation. The first is found in Genesis 1:27 which reads: "So God created humankind in his image, in the image of God he created them; male and female he created them." But then, in Genesis chapter two verse twenty-one reads: "So the Lord God caused a deep sleep to fall upon the man, and he slept; then he took one of his ribs and closed up its place with flesh. And the rib that the Lord God had

220

taken from the man he made into a woman and brought her to the man." In Chapter one of Genesis, God created the male and the female at the same time, whereas in Chapter two, the writer distinctly says that the man was created first, and the woman was created as a result of the man having been created first. Paul's writing then, in using the word 'head' is referring to the second creation narrative where man is created first, as in the *source* of the woman's creation. Understanding the theological and exegetical meaning of the word "head" as *Kephale*, or source, give us not only the proper meaning to Paul's text, but helps the family structure to understand their true relational roles. Before going further, it must be noted the word *Kephale* not only means "source," or the one who was born first, but it also means the one who is purposed to protect or defend another; and in the truest sense, the male is purposed to protect his mate.

With all that's been stated, we now come to the heart of this article. Men do have roles and responsibilities in the family. We are meant to be strong, protective, caring, loving, and yes even sensitive, but also a partner in the relationship. Many of the problems that men face as it relates to relationships, and I might add, why there are so many damaged relationships resulting in fatherless children, is when men try to do more than what the biblical relationship calls for. Just as Jesus lived his role or responsibility as the revealed presence of God, and just as Jesus humbled Himself unto God, we get the perfect example of how abiding in our roles is not diminutive in nature, but in fact it honors our purpose for being. When men purpose to dominate or rule women, when they purpose to be dictatorial always having their way, it causes all kind of problems in the relationship and within the family. Too often what causes stress to many men is that when they don't get their way, they determine that they're not being a "real man." What adds to that narrative is when women state I don't want a man who won't be a man, often meaning, I want a man to lead me. The problem with both narrow minded opinions or beliefs, as stated previously, is why does anyone have to dominate another in order to feel they are respected, but likewise, why does anyone need to be dominated in order to feel they are loved? In both cases, men and women are in error, because God never planned it that way. God put man and woman together as partners, and partners is the definition of the Hebraic word "helpmeet" as found in the King James Translation.

Here's the point to this article, men being men are fully men by being who God called them to be. A man being a man has nothing to do with how much you own, how many degrees you have earned, how many people report to you, or certainly, what individual you have under your control at home; it's about *Whose* we are and living in our God-given purpose. When men release the stress of living up to cultural, familial or even historical misunderstandings of leadership in the home, and embrace God's perspective of unity, partnership and oneness, the battles that too often are destructive to the relationship and to the family begin to end. When men are men it's because we have learned that everyone has a right to think, be, try, say and even fail; even if we don't agree with them.

God meant for all of His children, male and female to be whole. Wholeness is a process, but being whole—or the process of being whole—I will argue finds its genesis from the answering and evaluation of one question that everyone must answer for themselves. *Why do I love myself?* Why do I love me, sets the foundations on how I treat myself, what I expect, what I refuse to allow as part of my life, as well as this, how I treat others. Self-love rooted from and in the love of God is what manhood is made out of. Where there is healthy self-love, there is what I call soul-prosperity. A prosperous soul is one that has as much peace in the good times as in the bad. Scripture says: "Beloved, I pray that all may go well with you and that you may be in good health, just as it is well with your soul." (3 John 1:2 NRSV) The Scripture speaks of individual wholeness as well as soul-prosperity first, that leads to inner health, resulting in healthier relationships and healthier families.

When it comes to a man being a man, we must cast off ill-defined images of what a real man is and center our focus on what God calls us to be. In God's calling, we find self-love, we receive self-respect, and we learn self-worth.

Bibliography

Hamilton, Thomas. Beulah Heights University, 2008.

V. Horsley, Richard A. 1 Corinthians, Abingdon New Testament Commentaries (Nashville: Abingdon Press, 1998), p. 153.

~Dedication~

Men of Redemptive Life Christian Fellowship

Men of Allen Temple A.M.E. Church

Men of Big Bethel A.M.E. Church

Men of New Bethel A.M.E. Church

All my Sons and Daughters in Ministry

Truth and Accurate Understanding

Every Man Needs...

Calvin Ellison, PhD

1. A personal relationship with his Creator - God.

2. A mentor.

3. A friend.

4. A protégé.

5. A field of responsibility.

6. A library.

7. A support team.

8. A specific, consistent routine.

9. A problem he is determined to solve.

Register for our dynamic 2019-20 Orchestral School Year! Don't miss the "Early Bird" Special Tuition Discount if paid-in-full by September 7th. Visit www.sinfo-nia.com for details. Follow us on Social Media @SinfoNia Orchestra!

New Media Direct will provide a station, provide production of commercials, broadcasts. Partners are required to: originate clients/sponsors to broadcast, advertise and support the station. New Media will train salespersons, program music and provide commercial production.

A Streaming Station (also known as internet). New Media directs all content (advertising, public and community service and ministry broadcasts) toward a local area or community. The idea is to have a station that's focused on happenings in the local area, i.e. community events, local sports and news activities worthy of reaching your community.

Establishing A Media Center. Broadcast/ministry media centers of radio streaming that informs, inspires and empowers local civic and faith-based organizations.

A Community Station. The station will serve all area organizations promoting important events and providing support air time as a good community servant. Many civic organizations are interested in 30-60 minute live broadcast 2-2 weeks a month at your normal broadcast fees.

Partnership Interests ?
Call New Media Direct Today at (404) 465-3388!

227

Made in the USA
Columbia, SC
15 September 2023

22921240R00133